Japanese Cooking for Health and Fitness

Japanese Cooking
for Health and Fitness

Kiyoko Konishi

Woodbury, New York • London • Toronto • Sydney

The following companies generously contributed cooking and serving utensils for use in photographs appearing in this book.

Aoyama Craft Musée
Bingoya
Denenchofu Doraku
Ginka-corner
Ginza-blume
Ginza Matsuya
Heiando

Keio Department Store
Kitchen House
Kosta Boda
Kottoya Karakusa
Kurashi no Utsuwa Hanada
Noritake Co., Ltd.
Orange House

Savoir Vivre
Seika Suda
Sony Plaza Store
Takahashi Shoji Co., Ltd.
Toshiba Corporation
Yukimura

Kikkoman Corporation
Kikkoman International, Inc.
JFC International, Inc.
Pacific Trading Co., Ltd.

First U.S. Edition 1984 by
Barron's Educational Series, Inc.

© Copyright 1983 GAKKEN CO., LTD., Tokyo

All inquiries should be addressed to:
Barron's Educational Series, Inc.
113 Crossways Park Drive
Woodbury, New York 11797

International Standard Book No. 0-8120-5561-6

Credits:

Book design
Go Michiyoshi
Kazuyo Nakamura

Photography
Aritoshi Nakasato

Editorial assistance
Genevieve Shulick

**Nutritional data and
dietary advice**
Fukiko Takeuchi
(Caloric Diet School)

PRINTED IN JAPAN
4567   GAK   987654321

Foreword

It is said that French food appeals to the tongue, that Chinese food is kindest to the stomach, and that Japanese food pleases the eye. But Japanese food satisfies the palate and stomach as well, for it is healthful and delicious in addition to beautiful.

In this book, Mrs. Konishi introduces wholesome Japanese home-cooking—the same good food she prepares for her own family. She is a conscientious cook who cares about nutrition and economy as well as taste and the special enjoyment of seasonal foods and fresh ingredients.

I had lived in Tokyo for more than a year before I began taking cooking lessons from Mrs. Konishi who had been teaching small groups of foreign women in her home for over ten years. Before joining her class, I liked Japanese food, but found it difficult to prepare at home. Japanese supermarkets and shops were a bewildering array of unfamiliar items with unreadable names. When I asked how to prepare a certain dish, or asked where a friend learned to cook, the reply was usually, "I learned from my mother." How were those of us without Japanese mothers to learn Japanese cooking? For many foreign women in Tokyo, Mrs. Konishi has played the role of Japanese mother in the kitchen, and she has made it possible for our families to enjoy Japanese cooking at home, in Japan or wherever we may be. She teaches the folklore of the kitchen, the feel, smell and taste of food. Mrs. Konishi's recipes are also precise and systematic. She uses a variety of cooking methods and ingredients, many of which are familiar to foreigners. Since it is only the way of putting them together that makes them Japanese, anyone can cook a Japanese meal just by following her detailed instructions and observing the photographs.

This type of cooking does not require exotic ingredients, nor does it require a number of new utensils. In most cases, your frying pans, saucepans and casseroles will be quite adequate, although the visual aspect of the finished product may be slightly different. Japanese food is usually served in small individual dishes rather than on a large plate, but you can improvise with custard cups, saucers and salad plates.

Japanese food is becoming increasingly well known throughout the world. Americans on the East and West Coasts can enjoy *sushi* bars. Elegant Japanese restaurants are now found in cities scattered around the globe. Even if you are familiar with the standard restaurant dishes such as *tempura, sukiyaki* or *teppan-yaki,* you will discover simpler and more typical dishes here. For example, *nabeyaki-udon* is seldom found in restaurants here, but it can easily be prepared at home with noodles (even thick spaghetti would do), broth, chicken, carrots, spinach, mushrooms and eggs. It is a filling, warming treat on a cold night, even though it is not cooked at the table like other *nabemono. Nabemono,* or one-pot dishes, are favorites with my family. We sometimes cook them on a camp stove since we do not have a tabletop gas burner. Other favorite dishes are "instant pickles," beansprout salad, *namasu* and other oil-free salads or *sunomono* (vinegared dishes).

The negative aspect of enjoying food is the necessity of watching our weight. Most people think of Japanese food as being light and non-fattening, but a Japanese meal accompanied by rice can be quite filling. However, it is usually high in vegetables, fish and carbohydrates, and low in meats and fat. Thus, it has many positive nutritional aspects. The calorie count in these recipes will be helpful to all those who, like me, are trying to keep their weight down. For each recipe, a nutritional breakdown is also provided. In most of these dishes, *shoyu* (Japanese soy sauce, light or dark) and salt are used sparingly.

Mrs. Konishi is a traditionalist in the kitchen, but in other areas she is a dynamic woman with an optimistic and open-minded outlook on life. When she began teaching, cooking was her tool for learning English and expanding her own horizons. Through her teaching, she has made her life and ours more interesting. She is a person who makes her dreams come true by her hard work and originality.

I am very pleased to see her book appear so that her good cooking ideas will be shared with an even wider range of people. Each one of you who uses this cookbook will share some of the fun of being in Mrs. Konishi's kitchen, and then the enjoyment of eating the meal.

Itadakimasu.

Susan F. Stirn

U.S. Embassy, Tokyo, 1983

Preface

Japanese cooking is presently enjoying popularity in many parts of the world because it is not only pleasant to the eye and delicious but is also highly regarded as health food. On what points is it good for health and fitness? How is it cooked and served in such a charming way? This is the book that can answer these questions.

The first reason that Japanese cooking is good for the health is that it contains only small amounts of oils and fat. This is primarily because fish and shellfish, rather than meat, are the main sources of animal protein. Fish tend to be not only lower in oil and cholesterol but also more easily digestible than meat. Additionally, products made from soybeans, a wonderful source of high-quality vegetable protein, are prominent in the diet. Seasonings such as soy sauce and *miso* (fermented soybean paste), indispensable in Japanese cooking, are consumed almost daily, and many other soybean products, such as *tofu,* appear in innumerable dishes. A second reason Japanese cooking is good for the health is that fresh vegetables which contain a lot of dietary fiber are used abundantly. The number of different vegetables used at any one meal and the quantity of vegetables as a ratio of the entire meal are very high. The fiber in fresh vegetables facilitates digestion, and the consumption of a large variety of vegetables at one time provides a rich combination of vitamins and minerals. It is an added bonus that fresh vegetables are generally inexpensive and help stretch the meal resulting in lower food costs. Happily, also, Japanese-style seasonings and sauces tend to be low in calories, and cooking methods tend to use less oil. These constitute an important third and fourth reason for recommending Japanese cooking.

Since every recipe has a calorie count per serving at the top of the page, we invite you to use it as an aid in regulating your caloric intake. The levels of sodium contained in the recipes are lower than ordinarily contained in Japanese recipes, and great care has been taken that the reduction in sodium will not spoil the authentic taste and aroma of Japanese cooking.

It is a characteristic of Japanese cooking that ingredients are prepared using methods which help preserve the freshness and enhance the natural taste and aroma of the ingredients and also preserve their natural colors. An excellent example is *sashimi* (fresh fish eaten raw). The cooking time of Japanese ingredients is also relatively short, and this helps retain vitamins and minerals. In those cases where Japanese cooking methods are most likely to be unfamiliar to people outside Japan, I have explained the techniques as precisely as possible along with reasons for each step in the process.

You will note that not very many traditional Japanese-style serving utensils appear in this book. We have intentionally displayed some food on Western dishes hoping you will understand that Japanese meals can be attractively served using Western dishes from your own kitchen.

Many people contributed to the publishing of this book. I would like to express my gratitude to Mr. Mamoru Ogita, Mrs. Michiko Kawakami and Mr. Hitoshi Yamada of the editorial staff at Gakken Co., Ltd. and to Mrs. Genevieve Shulick who spent numerous hours checking the English, and who is herself a gourmet and fluent speaker of Japanese. The photographs appearing here are the labors of a superior photographer, Mr. Aritoshi Nakasato, whose camera work captures the beauty and suggests to the eye the deliciousness of Japanese cooking.

I dedicate this book to my husband, Kiyoharu Konishi, who helped plan and bring this book to fruition.

Contents

How to Use This Book

The recipes contained in this book include only dishes typically cooked in the Japanese home.

Calorie Count and Nutritional Information

As an aid for dieters, a calorie count appears beside each recipe along with data on the quantity of carbohydrates (excluding dietary fiber), protein and fats (oils and solid fats) contained in that dish. The data are for one portion, not the entire recipe. The data shown were calculated on the basis of the latest Japanese food composition tables. In the back of the book there is a sample menu plan for health and fitness using recipes in this book and advice for dieters. You may also find useful the special five-page section on entertaining with Japanese dishes. For your reference, we have added a glossary, with photographs, of major ingredients used in Japanese cooking as well as a supplementary section containing nutritional data on Japanese ingredients.

Presentation of Recipes

For each recipe there is a color photograph of the finished dish and, appearing with it, preparation and cooking instructions introduced in detail. For particularly complex preparations, small photographs have been added to demonstrate technique. Each recipe serves four people.

Weights and Measures

The weights and measures used in the list of ingredients and cooking instructions for each recipe are given in both the metric and standard American-British system of pounds and ounces. British cooks measure many more items by weight than do Americans, who prefer cup measurements for items such as rice, flour, chopped vegetables, and so on. When following the recipes, use the measurement you are most comfortable with.

Liquid measurements present more of a problem when a book is to be used by cooks in different countries. The Japanese cup, for example, measures 200 ml, whereas the American cup is 236 ml, the British cup is 284 ml, and the Australian cup is 250 ml. Since most of the ingredients measured in these recipes are of small quantities, these differences should not be a problem for cooks in any country. However, in dealing with quantities over 4 cups, we suggest you use the following conversion chart:

Liquid Measures—Conversion Chart (Cup Measures)

American Cup (in book)	United Kingdom Adjusts to:	Australia Adjusts to:
4 cups (2 pints)	1½ pints + 3 tablespoons	1½ pints − 3 tablespoons

A Note on Ingredients

These recipes require very few special ingredients; you can prepare many of these dishes using ingredients available in your local market. For a description of special Japanese ingredients, see pages 98-103. In addition, note the following:

- Measurements for carrots are given in ounces and grams. For cooks unused to measuring carrots this way, note that a large carrot weighs 4 ounces.

- Japanese cooks have a wider variety of onion-type plants to cook with. When selecting scallions, look for long ones with lengthy white parts. Green onions are mature scallions with a bulbous end, generally available in the spring.

- Japanese mustard is very strong, prepared without vinegar or spices. You may substitute any hot mustard without vinegar.

- Ginger juice appears as an ingredient in several recipes. To make juice, peel and grate fresh ginger, then squeeze out the juice.

RICE DISHES

Rice is a staple grain as well as a principal food in the Japanese daily diet. It is customarily prepared plain and eaten in combination with other dishes.

The kind of rice eaten is the short-grained variety which is grown in wetland paddies and becomes moderately soft and sticky when cooked. It is pleasant to the palate and delicious even without anything added. Therefore, when preparing Japanese rice dishes, it is highly recommended that short-grained rice be used rather than the long-grained variety commonly used in Western cooking.

In addition to being eaten plain, rice in Japan is also made into a wide variety of other dishes. One representative dish is *sushi,* which is rice flavored with a vinegar mixture, then topped, rolled, mixed or pressed together with raw fish or shellfish, egg, vegetables and so on. Typical of home-style dishes are rice boiled or steamed with various ingredients and seasonings (*takikomi-gohan*) or boiled plain and put into a serving dish, then topped with cooked meat or vegetables and served as a main dish (*donburi*). It is also cooked up as a soft gruel (*kayu*) or is boiled in soup along with meat and vegetables. For a simple snack, plain rice is put into a rice bowl and Japanese green tea or soup stock poured over (*ocha-zuke*).

There is hardly a meat, fish, or vegetable that is incompatible with the flavor of Japanese rice. Therefore, the possibilities for combining ingredients are many.

Noteworthy about rice are its low oil content and the energy which it provides. It also contains a good balance of essential amino acids indispensable to the human body (those eight types of amino acids which the body must take in from food). Compared to other grains, it can be said to have an excellent composition of protein. Since, however, its overconsumption can become a source of excess pounds, it should be eaten in moderation.

Hand-wrapped Sushi

CALORIES	743
PROTEIN	43.8g
FATS	12.2g
CARBOHYDRATES	104.2g

Of the many varieties of *sushi,* this is perhaps the easiest to make at home. Each person wraps his own, so the style is informal and best reserved for family and friends. The combination of rice, seafood and vegetables gives it a high nutritional value and low calorie content in proportion to volume.

Cooking time: 1 hour, plus 1 hour for draining rice

Ingredients
2 ounces (50g) fresh ginger
2½ cups (20 ounces) short-grained rice
3 inch (8cm) square piece dried kelp (*konbu*)
7 cups water
2 tablespoons *sake* or dry white wine
3 eggs
1½ teaspoons vegetable oil
8 medium shrimp
1 small cucumber, about 3 ounces (80g)
8 green *shiso* leaves, or use watercress, endive or chicory
4 ounces (100g) fresh tuna, reddish part
10 ounces (100g) fresh sea bream fillet
4 ounces (100g) smoked salmon
8 to 10 sheets dried laver (*nori*), about 8 x 7 inches (20 x 18cm)
1 tablespoon powdered or freshly grated Japanese green horseradish (*wasabi*)
½ lemon or lime (optional)
2 ounces (50g) salmon roe

To pickle ginger: 1 tablespoon sugar, ¼ teaspoon salt, 4 tablespoons rice vinegar or slightly diluted cider vinegar
To season rice: 5 tablespoons rice vinegar or slightly diluted cider vinegar, 2 tablespoons sugar, 2 teaspoons salt
To season eggs: 2 teaspoons sugar, ½ teaspoon *mirin*, pinch of salt
For dipping: 2 tablespoons soy sauce (½ tablespoon per person)

Preparation and Cooking
1. Mix thoroughly ingredients for pickling ginger. Peel ginger and slice paper-thin. Soak in boiling water for a few seconds. Drain. Put into pickling mixture immediately and leave at least 30 minutes. Drain before use.

2. Rinse rice 3 to 4 times or until water becomes almost clear, stirring gently by hand. Drain in colander for 1 hour.

3. Wipe *konbu* lightly with damp dish towel to clean; if powdery white substance can be seen on surface, do not wipe it off.* Cut into 4 pieces crosswise with scissors.

*This natural white substance is an essence of the *konbu* which forms as *konbu* dries. It imparts a good flavor to food with which it is cooked.

To rinse rice, stir gently by hand, until water becomes almost clear.

4. Combine rice, water, *sake* or dry white wine, and *konbu* in pot. Cover and bring to boil over high heat. Just before the water begins to boil up, take out *konbu*. Reduce heat to low and boil 15 minutes. Turn off heat and steam 10 minutes. Using wet wooden spatula, mix rice with folding motion from the bottom up to make it fluffy. Insert dry dish towel under lid to absorb excess moisture.

Just before the water begins to boil up, take out *konbu*.

After turning off heat and steaming, mix with folding motion.

Insert dry dish towel under lid and let stand 10 minutes more.

5. While rice is draining and subsequently being cooked, make remaining preparations in the following order.

a) Mix ingredients for seasoning cooked rice, stirring until sugar and salt dissolve.

b) Mix eggs lightly with chopsticks or fork, but do not beat. Add seasoning for eggs and mix well. Heat regular frying pan with oil, put in egg mixture, and sauté like an omelet, making it as even as possible all over. Cool and cut into 3 x ½ inch (8 x 1cm) bars.

c) Peel shrimp, but leave tails attached. Remove veins by inserting toothpick under vein at center of back and pulling up gently. If shrimp suitable for eating raw are not available, cook as follows. Stick fine skewer through each from head to tail on the stomach side to prevent curling when boiled. Boil in small amount of water with pinch of salt and dash of *sake* or dry white wine for 2 to 3 minutes. Drain. When half-cooled, remove skewers, twisting them as you pull them out.

d) Rub cucumber between your palms with a pinch of salt to soften, and rinse. Cut into thin strips about ½ inch (1cm) across and 3 inches (8cm) long. If seeds are tough, scoop them out.

e) Rinse green *shiso* leaves and pat dry.

f) Cut tuna, sea bream and smoked salmon into the same sized or slightly thinner pieces than the cucumber.

g) If *nori* is already toasted, cut into quarters. If not toasted, pass 2 sheets at a time back and forth quickly over medium flame (about 12 to 13 seconds or until slightly crispy). Cut into quarters.

h) Put *wasabi* into tiny jar with a lid, add ½ to 1 teaspoon water, and mix well. Turn jar upside down to enhance hot flavor. Cut lemon or lime, if using, into wedges.

6. When rice is well done, transfer right away to big shallow container (preferably wooden as wood absorbs moisture from hot rice and makes it tasty); pour seasonings on rice all at one time, and mix gently but quickly with wet wooden spatula. Immediately cool rice to room temperature by fanning continuously with fan. Quick cooling makes rice shiny and less starchy. Cover container with damp dish towel until use to prevent drying.

Transfer cooked rice quickly to large container. Pour mixed seasonings over it.

7. Arrange fish, egg, vegetables and condiments attractively on large platter. Put rice into serving bowl with 1 to 2 small flat spatulas. Place both along with *nori* and soy sauce on dining table.

With wet spatula, mix in seasonings quickly with chopping motion; do not mash.

Serving

Put ½ tablespoon of soy sauce per person onto small plates so that each person can serve himself, as shown in photographs below. Each person may choose ingredients of his own choice to wrap inside the *nori,* but in order to fully savor the delicious flavors of a variety of fish and shellfish, try wrapping one of each variety along with a vegetable. A squeeze of lemon or lime goes well with the salty taste of salmon roe and smoked salmon. Be careful not to overuse *wasabi,* which is very hot.

Put about 1 tablespoon of *sushi* rice on sheet of *nori,* as shown in photograph.

Put on ingredients and condiments of choice and wrap in *nori.*

Hold wrapped *sushi* in hand, dip lightly into soy sauce and eat.

Advice for Weight-watchers

Hand-wrapped *sushi* is a dish you can enjoy with friends, and in this kind of environment you can easily overeat. Since over half of the calories of *sushi* come from the rice, you can cut down on calories and still enjoy a balanced delicious meal. Just reduce the amount of rice by half each time you roll a piece. With less rice, you will notice how the delicious flavor of the other ingredients comes through more fully. *Sushi* connoisseurs prefer *sushi* with small proportions of rice.

Varieties of Sushi

Sushi is rice which is flavored with a vinegar mixture, and then to it fish, shellfish, vegetables, eggs, and so forth are variously added.

Sushi's origins are exceedingly old. In early times, people would preserve fish by salting and packing them between layers of rice. The fish fermented naturally and were tinged with an acidic flavor. At this point in time, *sushi* was still a sort of pickled fish.

Gradually, however, it developed into a dish in its own right divorced of the pickling function, but, in lieu of the acid generated by fermentation, vinegar came to be added to the rice.

Sushi variously reflects the local color of Japan as the ways of adding flavor to the vinegared rice and of making the *sushi*, selection of ingredients, and so on, differ by region. When the word "*sushi*" is used, it most commonly refers to *nigiri*- or hand-formed *sushi*. The history of this *sushi* is comparatively short, having first been made in the early period of the 19th century using fresh fish and shellfish from Tokyo Bay. Even today, hand-formed *sushi* is referred to as *Edo-mae-zushi* (Edo being Tokyo's former name).

In addition to the *sushi* displayed in the photographs, there are numerous others. The main varieties are:

BO-ZUSHI—Rice formed into a bar shape and topped with flavored fish;

SUGATA-ZUSHI—Rice topped with preflavored fish, such as sweetfish (*ayu*) or small sea bream, in such a way as to maintain the shape of the fish;

CHIRASHI-ZUSHI—Rice to which flavored vegetables are added, fish or shellfish sometimes being included also (see page 14 for one example);

MUSHI-ZUSHI—*Chirashi-zushi* steamed and served hot;

INARI-ZUSHI—*Abura-age* (thin deep-fried *tofu*) boiled in a sweet sauce and stuffed with rice.

Hand-formed *Sushi* (*nigiri-zushi*) and Rolled *Sushi* (*maki-zushi*)

Hand-formed *sushi* is vinegared rice formed into small mouth-sized rectangular blocks, swiped with a dab of *wasabi* (Japanese green horseradish), then topped with extremely fresh raw fish or shellfish. Hand-formed *sushi* shown here are squid, tuna (both pink and red meat), sea bream, ark shell, squilla (*shako*), a variety of eel (*anago*), a variety of yellowtail (*hamachi*), shrimp, *sushi*-style fried egg, a fish of the herring family (*kohada*), salmon roe, and sea urchin roe (*uni*). Rolled *sushi* is vinegared rice rolled up inside a sheet of *nori* (dried laver) with many kinds of ingredients, such as *kampyo* (dried gourd strips), raw tuna, and cucumber, placed in the center of the rice before rolling.

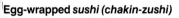

Egg-wrapped *sushi* (*chakin-zushi*)

Precooked and preflavored vegetables, such as Chinese black mushrooms and flaked fish, are mixed with vinegared rice (*chirashi-zushi* variety) and then wrapped decoratively inside a thinly fried layer of Japanese-style fried egg.

Box-molded or Pressed *Sushi* (*hako-zushi* or *oshi-zushi*)

Rice is pressed into a wooden box to make this *sushi*. Ingredients commonly used as topping are fish, squid, parboiled shrimp, *sushi*-style fried egg, boiled Chinese black mushrooms, barbecued eel, and so on.

Sushi Rice Mixed with a Colorful Variety of Vegetables

CALORIES 680
PROTEIN 16.3g
FATS. 9.2g
CARBOHYDRATES 127.0g

This is a home-style *sushi* which evokes a feeling of spring. Various ingredients are mixed with vinegared rice, then the rice is decorated on top with items added for color. It can also be topped with the types of fish and shellfish used for *sashimi*. If clear soup is served also, this will make a superb meal.

Preparation and Cooking

1. Rinse rice, drain in colander for 1 hour, and cook as explained in recipe for "Hand-wrapped Sushi," steps 2 to 4 and 6, pages 11-12.

2. While rice is draining and subsequently being cooked, prepare other ingredients in the following order.

a) Wet *kampyo* and rub between your palms with a pinch of salt to soften. Wash off salt, soak in warm water about 20 minutes, then boil in fresh water for about 10 minutes, or until tender. Drain and boil again in seasoning for *kampyo* over medium heat until semi-translucent and evenly brown all over and almost all liquid has been absorbed. Drain and cut crosswise into ½ inch (1cm) lengths.

b) Soak dried mushrooms in warm water for 10 to 15 minutes, or until tender. Remove stems and cut tops into fine strips.

c) Peel lotus root. Slice thinly crosswise, then cut each slice into pieces ½ inch (1cm) across. If lotus slices are less than 1½ inches (4cm) in diameter, use whole. Soak for 5 minutes in water containing 1 teaspoon vinegar to prevent discoloring. Drain.

d) Soak *abura-age* in boiling water for 1 minute. Pat dry. Cut in half lengthwise, then cut both pieces again crosswise into fine strips.

e) Cut carrot into 1 inch (2.5cm) long fine strips.

f) Boil mushrooms, lotus root, *abura-age* and carrot in their seasonings for 10 to 15 minutes over medium heat.

Cut mushrooms, *abura-age* and carrot into fine strips.

g) Stir eggs, add seasonings, and mix well. Sauté into several paper-thin sheets as follows. Grease frying pan with oil-dipped cotton or tissue paper, heat well and put about a quarter of egg mixture in, or enough to just cover the pan very thinly. If too much is poured in, pour excess back into bowl containing eggs. It will cook in a moment, so turn it over, using a wide spatula and your fingers, and cook only one second, then remove quickly from pan, and transfer to cutting board. Repeat this procedure until mixture is used up. Lay sheets on top of one another and cut into 1 inch (2.5cm) long fine strips.

Boil these cut ingredients along with lotus root in cooking broth and seasonings. Set aside until step 3.

h) Put snow peas into boiling water containing ¼ teaspoon salt and cook 2 to 3 minutes. Drain, and cut diagonally into fine strips.

i) Cut toasted *nori* into fine strips with scissors.

3. Drain off broth from mushrooms, *abura-age,* carrot and lotus root. Mix these along with *kampyo* into warm *sushi* rice. Do not mash.

Drain off broth and add these along with *kampyo* to warm rice.

Serving

Put mixed rice in a big bowl or into individual bowls. Garnish with egg strips, snow peas, *nori* and pickled ginger on top.

Cooking time: 1 hour, plus 1 hour to drain rice

Ingredients

2½ cups (20 ounces) short-grain rice

7 cups water

3 inch (8cm) piece dried kelp (*konbu*)

2 tablespoons *sake* or dry white wine

1 ounce (25g) dried gourd strips (*kampyo*)

1 cup *dashi* (page 26)

2 tablespoons sugar

2 tablespoons soy sauce

1 tablespoon *mirin*

4 dried Chinese black mushrooms

4 ounces (100g) lotus root

2 sheets thin deep-fried tofu (*abura-age*)

4 ounces (100g) carrot

2 eggs

1 teaspoon vegetable oil

1 ounce (25g) snow peas

½ sheet dried laver (*nori*), about 8 x 7 inches (20 x 18cm)

1 tablespoon pickled ginger cut into fine strips (page 11)

To boil *kampyo*: 1 cup *dashi* (page 26), 2 tablespoons sugar, 2 tablespoons soy sauce, 1 tablespoon *mirin*

To boil *abura-age*: soaking water from mushrooms plus enough *dashi* (page 26) to make 1 cup liquid, 1½ tablespoons sugar, 1½ tablespoons soy sauce, ⅓ teaspoon salt, 1 tablespoon *mirin*

To season eggs: 1 teaspoon sugar, pinch of salt

Rice Topped with Ground Chicken, Eggs and Green Peas

CALORIES 762
PROTEIN 30.6g
FATS. 19.4g
CARBOHYDRATES . . 105.4g

Rice Topped with Beef

CALORIES 658
PROTEIN 23.7g
FATS. 14.2g
CARBOHYDRATES . . . 99.6g

Cooking time: 40 minutes, plus 30 minutes for soaking rice

Ingredients

2½ cups (20 ounces) short-grained rice
7 cups water
10 ounces (300g) ground chicken
4 eggs
2 cups green peas, fresh or frozen
½ teaspoon salt
1 tablespoon pickled ginger cut into fine strips

To season meat: 1 tablespoon sugar, 1 tablespoon soy sauce, 1 tablespoon *sake* or dry white wine, 1 teaspoon ginger juice
To season eggs: 1 tablespoon sugar, 1 teaspoon soy sauce, ⅓ teaspoon salt, 1 tablespoon *sake* or dry white wine

Rice Topped with Ground Chicken, Eggs and Green Peas

Diners will be impressed by the pretty colors of this dish. It is also nutritionally balanced and can be made into a simple meal by the addition of a plain soup or drink. Boiled spinach or green beans can be used in lieu of green peas.

Preparation, Cooking and Serving

1. Rinse rice 3 to 4 times or until water becomes almost clear, stirring gently by hand. Soak in water for 30 minutes or longer in the pot in which it will be cooked.
2. Cover pot and bring water to boil over high heat. When it begins to simmer, reduce heat to low and boil 15 minutes. Turn off heat and steam 15 minutes. Using a wet wooden spatula, mix rice with folding motion from the bottom up to make it fluffy. Insert dry dish towel under lid to absorb excess moisture.
3. While rice is being cooked, prepare other ingredients in the following order.
a) Bring seasonings for meat to a boil, add meat and cook 3 to 4 minutes until well done, but still slightly moist, breaking up meat with chopsticks or fork.
b) In a small shallow saucepan, mix eggs well with chopsticks or whisk, but do not beat. Add seasonings for eggs and mix well. Cook over very low heat, stirring constantly from the beginning with 4 chopsticks or fork to break up lumps as they form. Cook until almost done but still moist, then remove from heat immediately. Scrape from pot using a rubber spatula.
c) Put green peas into boiling water containing ½ teaspoon salt and cook until well done. Drain and cool quickly.
4. Fill large rice bowls halfway with hot rice. Divide surface of the rice into 3 triangles, and fill triangles with ground chicken, egg, and green peas, completely covering the surface. Put several fine strips of ginger in the center.

Cooking time: 30 minutes, plus 30 minutes for soaking rice

Ingredients

2½ cups (20 ounces) short-grained rice
7 cups water
10 ounces (300g) sliced beef (shoulder or rump)
4 long scallions

To season meat: 4 tablespoons water, 3½ tablespoons *mirin*, 3½ tablespoons soy sauce

Rice Topped with Beef

Here beef and scallions are sweetly flavored by cooking in soy sauce and *mirin,* then put atop bowls of rice. Despite having to cook the rice, you can still make the dish very simply and quickly. The results are more delicious when marbled beef is used.

Preparation, Cooking and Serving

1. Rinse, soak, and cook rice as explained in recipe for "Rice Topped with Ground Chicken, Eggs and Green Peas," steps 1 and 2.
2. While rice is being cooked, cut beef into 1½ inch (4cm) squares and scallions crosswise into 1 inch (2.5cm) lengths.
3. Bring seasonings for beef to boil. Put in beef and cook about 2 minutes, or until done. Add scallions and turn off heat.
4. Fill large rice bowls halfway with hot rice, and put beef on top. Pour equal amounts of remaining soup over the surface. Serve hot.

Rice Cooked with Green Peas

CALORIES 481
PROTEIN 11.8g
FATS. 1.8g
CARBOHYDRATES 96.8g

Rice Cooked with Chicken and Vegetables

CALORIES 598
PROTEIN 23.7g
FATS. 11.8g
CARBOHYDRATES 96.8g

Cooking time: 30 minutes, plus 30 minutes for soaking rice

Ingredients
2½ cups (20 ounces) short-
  grained rice
7 cups water
1½ cups green peas, fresh or
  frozen
2½ teaspoons salt
2 tablespoons *sake* or dry white
  wine

Cooking time: 50 minutes, plus 30 minutes for draining rice

Ingredients
2½ cups (20 ounces) short-
  grained rice
7 cups water
4 dried Chinese black mushrooms
4 ounces (100g) carrot
7 ounces (200g) chicken (breast or
  thigh), bones and skin removed
2 sheets thin deep-fried bean curd
  (*abura-age*)
2 tablespoons *sake* or dry white
  wine
1 teaspoon soy sauce

Broth: 1 cup soaking water from
  mushrooms, 2 teaspoons sugar,
  1 teaspoon salt, 3 tablespoons
  soy sauce, 2 tablespoons *sake*
  or dry white wine

Rice Cooked with Green Peas

When the season for green peas rolls around, you will surely want to try this rice dish, which is lightly flavored with salt. It will look very appetizing served alongside meat or fish. A delicious dish can also be turned out using frozen green peas.

Preparation and Cooking

1. Rinse rice 3 to 4 times or until water becomes almost clear, stirring gently by hand. Soak in water for 30 minutes or longer in the pot in which it will be cooked.

2. Five minutes before cooking, sprinkle green peas with 1 teaspoon salt.

3. Leaving the rice in its soaking water, mix in *sake* and remaining salt. Spread green peas over the rice. Cover and bring to boil over high heat. When it simmers, reduce heat to low and boil 15 minutes. Turn off heat and steam 15 minutes. Using wet wooden spatula, mix rice with folding motion from the bottom up to make it fluffy. Insert dry dish towel under lid to absorb excess moisture.

Rice Cooked with Chicken and Vegetables

This is a highly nutritious rice dish with a rich soy sauce flavor. You need not limit yourself to the ingredients used here. In Japan, rice is also cooked with vegetables, fish and shellfish which are in season or which evoke some feeling of the time of year.

Preparation and Cooking

1. Rinse rice 3 to 4 times or until water becomes almost clear, stirring gently by hand. Drain in colander for 30 minutes or more.

2. Soak dried mushrooms in enough warm water to just cover them (about 1 cup) for 10 to 15 minutes, or until tender, then squeeze slightly. Remove stems and cut tops into fine strips.

3. Julienne carrot into 1 inch (2.5cm) lengths (cut crosswise into 1 inch (2.5cm) sections, slice each section thinly lengthwise, then cut each of these slices again lengthwise into fine strips).

4. Cut chicken into 1 inch (2.5cm) squares.

5. Soak *abura-age* in boiling water for 1 minute to remove oil, and pat dry. Cut in half lengthwise, then again crosswise into ¼ inch (0.5cm) wide strips.

6. Boil mushrooms and carrot strips in cooking broth for chicken and vegetables until half-done, or for about 5 minutes, then add chicken and *abura-age*. Continue to boil 3 to 4 minutes until everything is done. Drain and set aside. Retain the soup.

7. Add 2 tablespoons *sake* and 1 teaspoon soy sauce to the retained soup above, then add enough water to bring the total amount of liquid to 7 cups. Put in rice and bring to boil over high heat. When broth simmers, reduce heat to low and boil 15 minutes. Turn off heat and let stand 15 minutes.

8. Reheat slightly the boiled chicken and vegetables from step 6. Using a wet wooden spatula, stir them into the rice with folding motion from the bottom up. Then insert a dry dish towel under lid to absorb excess moisture.

SOUPS

Soup is an important entry on any basic menu of Japanese cooking. It is generally served along with the main part of the meal rather than prior to it, as in Western serving. Its main function in the meal is to facilitate the eating of the rice. Because it is sipped between bites of the various dishes, it also enhances the flavor of the entire meal. Soup is also occasionally served near the end of a meal to complete it and remove any unpleasant tastes remaining in the mouth.

The methods of preparing Japanese soups are various. The key consideration in all soups, however, is to create a sense of season through choice of seasonal ingredients, color of ingredients, and so on. Special effort is also made to achieve harmony among flavor, aroma and coloring.

Japanese soups can be generally divided into two types—clear soups and *miso* soups.

Clear soups (*sumashi-jiru*): Clear in color, they are generally made by flavoring *dashi* (bonito fish stock) with salt and a small amount of soy sauce. The two major ingredients of basic *dashi* are *katsuobushi* (shaved bonito fish flakes) and *konbu* (kelp). Since the flavor is decided mainly by the quality of the *dashi,* one should use high-quality *katsuobushi* and *konbu.* In addition to bonito fish stock, stocks made from other fish, shellfish or meat are also used occasionally to make clear soups.

For solid ingredients to serve in clear broth, fish or shellfish, meat (mainly lean chicken), egg, *tofu,* seasonal vegetables, and so on, are used. Some condiment with pleasant aroma is generally added just before serving.

Miso soups (*miso-shiru*): *Miso* (fermented bean paste) is added to *dashi* to create this soup. It regularly appears at everyday meals but is not generally served to guests.

Miso is made all over Japan. Consequently, the flavor of *miso* soup differs a little by region and family. For solid ingredients, one generally chooses two items from among vegetables in season, shellfish, seaweeds, *tofu, abura-age* (thin, deep-fried *tofu*), and so on.

Clear Soups

Clear Soup with Shrimp and Okra

CALORIES 24
PROTEIN 5.2g
FATS 0.2g
CARBOHYDRATES 0.2g

Clear Soup with Clams

CALORIES 12
PROTEIN 1.2g
FATS 0.1g
CARBOHYDRATES 0.5g

Japanese Egg-drop Soup with Chicken and Carrot

CALORIES 90
PROTEIN 7.9g
FATS 5.6g
CARBOHYDRATES 0.9g

Miso Soups

Miso Soup with Pork and Scallions

CALORIES 125
PROTEIN 5.1g
FATS 9.6g
CARBOHYDRATES 3.7g

Miso Soup with Tofu and Shiitake Mushrooms

CALORIES 52
PROTEIN 4.2g
FATS 2.3g
CARBOHYDRATES 4.5g

Miso Soup with Long White Radish and Green Beans

CALORIES 36
PROTEIN 2.4g
FATS 1.0g
CARBOHYDRATES 4.1g

Cooking time: 20 minutes

Ingredients
4 medium shrimp or 8 to 12 small
2 pieces okra
1 inch (2.5 cm) square piece lemon
　rind
4 cups *dashi* (page 26)
⅔ teaspoon salt
1 teaspoon soy sauce

Cooking time: 15 minutes

Ingredients
4 large or 8 medium clams in the
　shell
4 inch (10cm) square piece dried
　kelp (*konbu*)
½ tender long scallion
1 inch (2.5cm) square piece lemon
　rind
4 cups water
⅔ teaspoon salt
1 tablespoon *sake* or dry white
　wine
¼ teaspoon soy sauce

Cooking time: 20 minutes

Ingredients
3 ounces (80g) chicken, bones and
　skin removed
1 ounce (25g) carrot
1 teaspoon salt
2 eggs
4 cups *dashi* (page 26)
1 teaspoon soy sauce

To season chicken: pinch of salt, 1
　teaspoon *sake* or dry white wine

Clear Soups

Clear soups are elegant soups. Special care should be given to the flavor, texture, color, shape, size and season of ingredients and to the overall beauty of their arrangement in the bowl. Garnishes with refreshing fragrances are added just before serving.

Clear Soup with Shrimp and Okra

1. Peel shrimp, but leave tails and last section of shell nearest the tail attached. Remove veins by inserting toothpick under vein at center of the back and pulling up gently.
2. Bring to boil small amount of water containing pinch of salt. Put in shrimp, boil 2 to 3 minutes or until done (time depending on size of shrimp) and drain.
3. Cut okra into ¼ inch (0.5cm) thick rounds.
4. Cut lemon rind into needle-fine strips.
5. Bring *dashi* to boil, then add salt. When salt has dissolved, add soy sauce. Put in okra and turn off heat.
6. Put one medium-sized shrimp or a few small ones into each soup bowl. Ladle in piping hot soup and serve immediately with 3 to 4 fine strips of lemon rind on top.

Clear Soup with Clams

1. Put clams into colander and immerse in salt water containing 1 teaspoon salt per cup of water. The water should almost cover the clams. Clams should be kept in a dark cool place until used.
2. Wipe *konbu* with damp dish towel to remove any sand, and cut crosswise into 4 pieces with scissors.
3. Cut scallion crosswise into paper-thin slices.
4. Cut lemon rind into needle-fine strips.
5. Just before cooking, rinse clams under running water.
6. Put clams and *konbu* into 4 cups water, and bring to boil. Just before water simmers, take out *konbu*. Remove scum, then add salt, *sake* and soy sauce. Continue to boil until clams open, then add scallion and turn off heat.
7. Put 1 to 2 clams into soup bowls, and ladle in the boiling hot soup. Add a few pieces of lemon rind.
Note: Clams which do not open when heated are not edible and should be picked out and thrown away.

Japanese Egg-drop Soup with Chicken and Carrot

1. Dice chicken and season with salt and *sake* or dry white wine.
2. Cut carrot crosswise into ¼ inch (0.5cm) rounds. Bring small amount of water containing ¼ teaspoon salt to a boil. Add carrot, cook about 2 minutes, and drain.
3. Mix eggs well, but lightly, with chopsticks or fork. Do not beat.
4. Bring *dashi* to boil over high heat. Add remaining salt, soy sauce, and chicken pieces quickly one by one. Reduce heat and boil 2 minutes. Add egg little by little, stirring constantly; the soup must be boiling at this stage. When final egg threads have formed, turn off heat immediately.
5. Place carrot in each soup bowl, and add piping hot soup.

Miso Soups

Miso soup is very healthful. We introduce three types—one with pork, another with *tofu,* and a third with seasonal vegetables. This soup goes well with Western food too, so we recommend you give it a try. The amount of *miso* you use depends on its saltiness—taste before adding full amount in recipe.

Miso Soup with Pork and Scallions

Cooking time: 15 minutes

Ingredients
3 ounces (80g) lean pork, thinly sliced
1 long scallion or 2 inches (5cm) leek
4 cups *dashi* (page 26)
3 to 4 tablespoons *miso*
2 teaspoons ginger juice

1. Cut pork into 1 inch (2.5cm) square pieces.
2. Slice scallion crosswise into ½ inch (1cm) lengths. If using leek, cut crosswise into thin rounds.
3. Bring *dashi* to boil, add pork, and boil about 2 minutes. Put *miso* onto ladle, immerse ladle in soup, and add broth little by little to the *miso,* stirring constantly with chopsticks until completely dissolved. Stir the dissolved *miso* back into the pot gradually, making sure there are no lumps. Finally, add scallion. Just after soup boils again, turn off heat. Do not overcook.*
4. Put boiling hot soup into soup bowls, stir in ½ teaspoon ginger juice per serving as condiment, and serve immediately.

Miso Soup with Tofu and Shiitake Mushrooms

Cooking time: 15 minutes

Ingredients
4 *shittake* or other fresh mushrooms
½ block *tofu*
4 cups *dashi* (page 26)
3 to 4 tablespoons *miso*

1. Remove stems from shiitake mushrooms, and cut tops into ½ inch (1cm) wide strips.
2. Dice *tofu* into small cubes.
3. Put mushrooms into *dashi* and bring to boil. Continue to boil for 1 minute then add *tofu.* Put *miso* onto ladle, immerse ladle in soup and add broth little by little to the *miso,* stirring constantly with chopsticks until completely dissolved. Stir the dissolved *miso* back into the pot gradually, making sure there are no lumps. Just after it boils again, turn off heat. Do not overcook.*
4. Put boiling hot soup into soup bowls and serve immediately.

Miso Soup with Long White Radish and Green Beans

Cooking time: 15 minutes

Ingredients
4 ounces (100g) long white radish
6 green beans
4 cups *dashi* (page 26)
3 to 4 tablespoons *miso*

1. Quarter long white radish, then slice each quarter thinly crosswise.
2. Remove strings from beans and cut into 1 inch (2.5cm) lengths.
3. Put radish into *dashi* and cook for 2 minutes. Add green beans and boil 2 minutes more. Finally, put *miso* onto ladle, immerse ladle in soup, and add broth little by little to the *miso,* stirring constantly with chopsticks until completely dissolved. Stir the dissolved *miso* back into the pot gradually, making sure there are no lumps. Just after it boils again, turn off heat. Do not overcook.*
4. Put boiling hot soup into soup bowls and serve immediately.

Note: Adding one sheet of *abura-age* (thin deep-fried *tofu*) to this recipe, if available, will greatly enhance its flavor. Soak *abura-age* in boiling hot water for 1 minute to remove oil, and pat dry, wiping off excess oil. Cut in half lengthwise, then again crosswise into fine strips, add to soup after green beans are cooked. Then add *miso.*

*After dissolving the *miso*, it is absolutely essential for you not to continue to cook the soup after it begins to boil again. If you do so, both the good aroma imparted by the *miso* and its original tasty flavor will be destroyed.

How to Make Dashi (Bonito Fish Stock)

Knowing how to make *dashi* is essential if you hope to turn out delicious Japanese dishes, such as clear soup, *miso* soup, boiled vegetable dishes, and dipping sauce for *tempura*. *Dashi* is equivalent to bouillon in Western cooking, so by all means try to master making it. The *dashi* introduced here is a high-grade *dashi* which combines the flavor of inosinic acid, which is the main essence of *katsuobushi* (bonito fish flakes), and the flavor of glutamic acid, which emanates from *konbu* (dried kelp). Because *dashi* has a high-quality taste without any particularly strong flavor or odor, it goes well with almost any kind of cooking. Wipe the *konbu* with a damp cloth, but do not wipe off the white powdery substance on the surface which forms as the *konbu* dries. Also, do not put a lid on the pot when boiling *dashi* or the broth will become cloudy and develop a bad odor, and you will not be able to produce a good soup.

Instant *Dashi*

There are two types. One is a dry pulverized form, and the other a condensed liquid. In either case, just add it to boiling water to get *dashi*. Instant *dashi* is especially convenient when in a hurry or when only a small quantity is needed. For more detail, refer to page 103 of "Glossary of Major Japanese Ingredients" under "*Katsuo-dashi* and *Konbu-dashi*."

Ingredients (to make 4 cups)
4¼ cups water
4 inch (10cm) piece dried kelp (*konbu*)
1 cup (5g) bonito fish flakes (*katsuobushi*)

Wipe the *konbu* with a damp cloth and cut into 4 pieces with scissors to allow flavor to escape.

Put 4 cups of water and *konbu* into pan and bring to boil over medium heat.

Immediately when water begins to boil, take out *konbu*. Do not overcook.

Add ¼ cup cold water to stop the boiling.

Add 1 cup *katsuobushi* all at once. When water boils again, turn off heat.

When *katsuobushi* has all sunk to the bottom, strain soup through cheesecloth-lined sieve or ordinary fine sieve.

Instant Miso and Instant Clear Soups

Instant *miso* and instant clear soups can be made very simply just by adding boiling water and stirring. These soups are made by special processing methods so as to approximate as closely as possible the taste of home-made soups. These instant soups can be used in everyday cooking, but are especially handy when guests arrive unexpectedly. They are also very useful to take along on camping trips or to stock as emergency rations.

Instant Miso Soup
The packets contain powdered *miso*, *wakame*, wheat gluten, *katsuobushi* powder, dried scallion, and so forth. They come in two types: red *(aka)* and white *(shiro)*, differentiated by the type of *miso* used.

Instant Clear Soup
The packets contain salt, dried mushrooms, powdered soy sauce, wheat gluten, *nori* (dried laver), *katsuobushi* powder, dried scallion, and so forth.

Japanese-style Vegetable Soup

CALORIES 186
PROTEIN 12.0g
FATS. 10.0g
CARBOHYDRATES 12.2g

Cooking time: 30 minutes

Ingredients
4 ounces (100g) burdock root,
   fresh or canned
1 teaspoon vinegar
1 white potato
4 ounces (100g) long white radish
   (*daikon*)
2 ounces (50g) carrot
1 long scallion
1 block *tofu*
4 *shiitake* or other fresh
   mushrooms
2 teaspoons vegetable oil or
   1 teaspoon each sesame and
   vegetable oils
4 ounces (100g) ground chicken
   or pork
6 cups *dashi* (page 26) or canned
   or homemade chicken stock
1 teaspoon salt
1½ tablespoons soy sauce
Seven-flavored cayenne (*shichimi*
   togarashi) (optional)

Cooking time: 30 minutes

Ingredients
7 ounces (200g) pork, thinly sliced
Same vegetables as for above
   recipe
6 cups water
5 to 6 tablespoons *miso*
4 *shiitake* or other fresh
   mushrooms
2 teaspoons ginger juice

Japanese-style Vegetable Soup

Long white radish, carrot, potato and burdock root are sautéed together with ground meat, then lightly flavored with salt and soy sauce. Finally, coarsely broken *tofu* is added. The vegetables of this dish contain abundant dietary fiber.

Preparation
1. Scrape burdock root, if fresh, with back of knife to remove brown thin skin, then shave diagonally into 1 inch (2.5cm) long, narrow thin chips as if you were sharpening a pencil. Soak right away in water containing 1 teaspoon vinegar for 3 to 4 minutes to prevent discoloring, then drain and rinse off vinegar.
2. Peel potato and quarter. Slice each quarter thinly, soak in water for 2 to 3 minutes to prevent discoloring, and drain.
3. Peel and slice long white radish and carrot into the same size pieces as the potato.
4. Cut scallion crosswise into ½ inch (1cm) lengths.
5. Break *tofu* coarsely into a colander to remove excess moisture.
6. Remove stems from mushrooms; cut tops into fine strips.

Cooking and Serving
1. Heat 2 teaspoons of oil in pot for 1 minute over high heat. Add ground meat and sauté until meat turns whitish, breaking it up with spatula to prevent lumps. Add long white radish, carrot, burdock root and potato, and continue to sauté for 2 to 3 minutes.
2. Add *dashi,* season with salt and soy sauce, and boil until vegetables are done, or about 5 minutes. Add mushrooms and *tofu* and boil 2 minutes more. Last, put in scallion and turn off heat right away.
3. Serve hot in soup bowls with a condiment such as *shichimi togarashi*.

Variation
Japanese-style Pork Soup

This is a *miso*-flavored soup containing an abundant quantity of vegetables. Since a delicious flavor emanates from the pork, no soup stock is necessary. Using pork meat with a little fat will make the dish more tasty.

Preparation and Cooking
1. Cut pork into 1 inch (2.5cm) lengths.
2. Cut vegetables as explained in recipe for "Japanese-style Vegetable Soup."
3. Boil long white radish, burdock root, and carrot in 6 cups water for 5 minutes, or until half-done, then add meat. When the color of the meat turns white, put in mushrooms, and cook 1 minute.
4. When everything is done, put *miso* onto ladle, immerse ladle in soup, and add broth little by little to the *miso,* stirring constantly with chopsticks until completely dissolved. Stir the dissolved *miso* back into the pot gradually, making sure there are no lumps. Boil 2 to 3 minutes. Finally, put in scallion and turn off heat.

Serving
Put piping hot soup into bowls, stir in ½ teaspoon ginger juice per serving as condiment, and serve immediately.

ONE-POT TABLE COOKING

In Japan there are many dishes containing meat, seafood and vegetables which are cooked at the table in a large common container, diners helping themselves while remaining ingredients continue to cook. As diners gather around the one cooking container, the atmosphere created is homey and intimate. In winter, the heat from the burner and the piping hot food warm the body and give one a sense of well-being.

There are various types of one-utensil table cooking. Two popular ones introduced here are *nabemono,* in which the ingredients are boiled and eaten from a common container, and *teppan-yaki*, in which the ingredients are grilled and then eaten directly.

One well-known *nabemono* is *sukiyaki,* a dish of beef, *tofu* and vegetables cooked in a rich soy sauce-based broth. In most other *nabemono,* ingredients are boiled in water or in a weak-flavored broth and eaten with condiments of one's choice. Although variously flavored, their preparation is simple. It is the combination of ingredients and their freshness and quality that are the deciding factors in determining the flavor of a dish.

Nabemono is most delicious eaten while the pot's ingredients are still cooking at the table. If, however, you have no cooking apparatus for use at the table, or if you wish to serve it during a season when it is too hot to cook at the table, it is acceptable to first cook the ingredients in the kitchen, then carry the container to the table.

One-pot table cooking is a healthy way of eating. The large variety of ingredients creates good nutritional balance, and the short cooking time for most ingredients helps preserve their nutrients. Since most dishes do not use oil, they are also low in calories. You may select ingredients of your own choice or reduce the quantity of ingredients. There will still be lots of broth to drink, which will leave the stomach feeling full. Since ingredients can be eaten freely from the main dish, however, dieters need to exercise self-control.

Sukiyaki

CALORIES 501
PROTEIN 35.5g
FATS 25.6g
CARBOHYDRATES 29.3g

Seared Beef with Flavorful Dipping Sauces
(shabushabu)

CALORIES 407
PROTEIN 30.8g
FATS. 22.0g
CARBOHYDRATES 21.1g

Preparation time: 20 minutes

Ingredients

14 ounces (400g) beef sirloin,
  tenderloin, or rump, sliced
  paper-thin
7 ounces (200g) devil's tongue
  jelly noodles (*shirataki*) or 1
  ounce (25g) Chinese bean
  thread noodles (*harusame*)
1 block *tofu*
8 *shiitake* or other fresh
  mushrooms
2 leeks or 7 to 8 long scallions
4 ounces (100g) fresh spinach
4 eggs (optional)
3 to 4 1-inch (2.5cm) beef suet
  cubes

Warishita broth: 3 tablespoons
  sugar, ¼ cup sake or dry white
  wine, ¼ cup *mirin*, ¼ cup soy
  sauce, ½ cup water

Utensils

Cast-iron skillet, flameproof
  shallow casserole, or electric
  skillet
Portable heating equipment with
  adjustable heat

Sukiyaki

It is hard to resist the succulent taste of beef cooked along with vegetables in a hearty broth of soy sauce, sugar, *sake* and sweet rice wine and then dipped into mouth-watering sauces. Sukiyaki's universal appeal has made it one of the most popular of Japanese dishes abroad.

Preparation

1. Cut meat into 3 inch (7.5cm) lengths.
2. Parboil *shirataki* in boiling water for 2 minutes. Cut into 4 inch (10cm) long pieces and drain in colander.
3. Cut *tofu* into 1 inch (2.5cm) cubes and drain.
4. Remove stems from mushrooms. If desired, carve out a crisscross design on top for decoration.
5. Cut leeks diagonally into ½ inch (1cm) thick slices, holding the knife at about a 45° angle to the length of the leek. If using scallions, cut crosswise in ordinary way into 2 inch (5cm) long pieces.

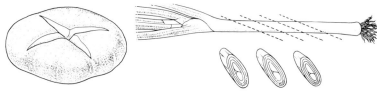

How to Cut Mushrooms Decoratively
Tilt the knife when cutting. The carved area should be V-shaped.

How to Cut a Leek
It is attractive when cut obliquely and flavor is absorbed well.

6. Cut spinach in half crosswise.
7. Arrange all ingredients attractively on large platter with serving chopsticks or fork.
8. Mix or heat ingredients for *warishita* broth thoroughly until sugar dissolves and place on dining table in small container.
9. Break 1 raw egg per person into individual bowls for diners to use as dipping sauce, if desired. Place at each diner's setting.

Cooking and Serving

1. Heat skillet on the dining table and sauté beef suet cubes until half-melted, greasing the pan evenly. Put in several slices of beef and sauté. When half-done, add ½ of *warishita* broth and equal amounts of other ingredients (usually watery items such as *tofu* and *shirataki* noodles are added first) as well as more beef.
2. The diner should mix the raw egg with chopsticks. As the food becomes done, each person serves himself from the skillet, dipping food into egg before eating, if desired.
3. Ingredients and broth should be added as needed. If amount of liquid is insufficient, add remaining *warishita* broth. If flavor becomes too strong, add water and adjust flavor as desired.

Note: If you are not able to cook *sukiyaki* at the table because you do not have the necessary utensils, select a casserole dish with a size that corresponds to the number of diners and cook the ingredients in it in the kitchen. When done, serve at the table. If cooking one time is not enough, repeat 2 to 3 times, or as necessary.

Advice for Weight Watchers
The calorie data indicated on page 30 are numerical values for rump meat. The figure for tenderloin is 455 calories, and for sirloin, 453 calories. There are some differences in the nutritional composition of beef based on country, raising conditions, and so on, so the data here should be construed only as a general indicator.

Preparation time: 30 minutes

Ingredients
1 block *tofu*
7 ounces (200g) devil's tongue jelly noodles (*shirataki*) or 1 ounce (25g) Chinese bean thread noodles (*harusame*)
2 leeks
8 *shiitake* or other fresh mushrooms
4 leaves Chinese cabbage
4 inch (10cm) square piece dried kelp (*konbu*)
14 ounces (400g) beef sirloin, tenderloin, shoulder or rump, sliced paper-thin

Sesame seed sauce: 4 tablespoons white sesame seeds, 1 tablespoon *miso*, 1 tablespoon sugar, 2 tablespoons *mirin*, 2 tablespoons rice vinegar or slightly diluted cider vinegar, 1 tablespoon *sake* or dry white wine, 4 tablespoons soy sauce, 1 teaspoon prepared Japanese mustard
Ponzu sauce: ½ cup lemon juice or commercial *ponzu**, ½ cup soy sauce, ½ cup water

Condiments
About 4 inch (10cm) thick section long white radish (*daikon*), peeled and grated (1½ tablespoons per serving)
2 long scallions, sliced paper-thin crosswise (½ tablespoon per serving)

Utensils
Mongolian-style pot or an iron, earthenware, electric or flameproof casserole pot
Portable heating equipment with adjustable flame

---

*Has a citric flavor

Seared Beef with Flavorful Dipping Sauces (*shabushabu*)

Water is brought to a boil in a large serving container. Diners put in one thin slice of beef at a time and, holding it with chopsticks, swish it back and forth for a few seconds in the boiling water until seared. It is then eaten with sauce and condiments of one's choice.

Preparation
1. Prepare dipping sauces. For sesame sauce, first toast seeds in a dry frying pan without oil over medium-to-high heat, shaking pan constantly from the beginning to prevent burning. When popping begins, transfer to a grinder or eathenware mortar, and grind until smooth with pestle while the seeds are still hot. Add all other ingredients for the sauce to the ground seeds, and mix well. For *ponzu* sauce, mix all ingredients together.
2. Prepare condiments.
3. Cut *tofu* into 1 inch (2.5cm) cubes and drain.
4. Parboil *shirataki* in boiling water for 2 minutes. Cut into 4 inch (10cm) long pieces and drain in colander. If using *harusame,* parboil in boiling water for 3 minutes, or soak in boiling water for 15 minutes. Drain and cut into 4 inch (10cm) long pieces.
5. Cut leeks diagonally into ½ inch (1cm) thick slices, holding the knife at about a 45° angle to length of leek.
6. Remove stems from mushrooms. If desired, carve out a crisscross design on top for decoration.
7. Cut Chinese cabbage leaves into 2 inch (5cm) square pieces.
8. Wipe *konbu* with damp dish towel to remove any sand, and cut into 4 pieces crosswise with scissors.
9. Arrange all ingredients attractively on large platter, taking into consideration colors and shapes, and place on dining table with serving fork or chopsticks.

Cooking and Serving
1. Put *konbu* into 5 to 6 cups water and bring to boil on dining table, or heat it first on the kitchen stove (this is quicker), and then transfer it to the heating apparatus on the dining table. When it simmers, take *konbu* out.
2. Each person prepares both kinds of dipping sauce in his own dipping bowls by mixing sesame or *ponzu* sauce with condiments (sesame with scallion and *ponzu* with scallion and/or radish). You can make two different types of dipping sauces in different bowls, or can alternate in the same bowl.
3. To the boiling water, add first the ingredients which take the longest time to cook, followed by the others. Add ingredients in equal amounts little by little, i.e., only a quantity sufficient for each person to sample a little at a time. Do not add all ingredients at once.
4. To cook the beef, take a slice of it with chopsticks or fondue fork, and wave it back and forth in the piping hot broth for a few seconds. When it is half-done, dip it into the dipping sauce and eat as is. You may help yourself to the other ingredients as you prefer.
5. While it is boiling, the soup should be skimmed occasionally with a ladle. Additional ingredients should be put into the pot so that equal amounts of each ingredient are always ready for eating. If the level of soup falls too low, add some boiling broth or boiling water.

Chicken and Vegetables Cooked in an Earthenware Container

CALORIES	486
PROTEIN	39.5g
FATS	30.0g
CARBOHYDRATES	12.5g

Meat, Seafood and Vegetables Cooked in an Earthenware Container

CALORIES 463
PROTEIN 57.3g
FATS. 17.0g
CARBOHYDRATES 16.7g

Preparation time: 50 minutes

Ingredients

2 pounds (800 to 900g) chicken, bones and skin attached

4 inch (10cm) square piece dried kelp (*konbu*)

2 tablespoons unrinsed raw rice, put into a 4 inch (10cm) square gauze or cheesecloth bag and cooked along with chicken (to remove chicken smell and enrich soup; optional)

4 leaves Chinese cabbage

4 ounces (100g) carrot

8 *shiitake* or other fresh mushrooms

1 block *tofu*

7 ounces (200g) devil's tongue jelly noodles (*shirataki*) or 1 ounce (25g) Chinese bean thread noodles (*harusame*)

2 leeks

Broth: 7 to 8 cups water, 1 teaspoon salt, ½ teaspoon sugar, 1 tablespoon *sake* or dry white wine

Ponzu sauce: ½ cup lemon juice or commercial *ponzu**, ½ cup soy sauce, ½ cup water

Condiments

About 4 inch (10cm) thick section long white radish, peeled and grated, then mixed with a couple dashes of ground red-pepper (1½ tablespoons per serving)

½ tender long scallion, sliced paper-thin crosswise (½ tablespoon per serving)

4 wedges lime or lemon (optional)

Seven-flavored cayenne (*shichimi togarashi*) or *sansho* powder

*Has a citric flavor

Chicken and Vegetables Cooked in an Earthenware Container

In this one-pot dish, ingredients are cooked in a refreshing, mild broth and eaten with condiments and citric sauce. The combination of chicken and vegetables provides high-quality protein and also is nutritionally well-balanced.

Preparation

1. Cut chicken into 1½ inch (4cm) square pieces. Put in big colander and pour boiling water on the chicken to remove blood and surface film.

2. Wipe *konbu* with damp dish towel to remove any sand, and cut into 4 pieces crosswise with scissors.

3. Put broth, then chicken, *konbu* and rice bag into wide earthenware pot or strong casserole dish, and bring to boil over low heat first, then medium heat on the kitchen stove. When it simmers, take out *konbu,* and boil for 30 minutes, skimming bubbles, scum and chicken fat off top of broth occasionally. While waiting for chicken, prepare other ingredients. When chicken is done, take out rice bag and transfer pot to the heating apparatus on the dining table for cooking.

4. Mix ingredients for dipping sauce and prepare condiments.

5. Cut Chinese cabbage leaves into 2 inch (5cm) square pieces.

6. Cut carrot crosswise into round slices about ½ inch (1cm) thick then carve slices into flower shapes, if desired.

7. Remove stems from mushrooms. If desired, carve a crisscross design on top for decoration.

8. Cut *tofu* into 1 inch (2.5cm) cubes and drain.

9. Parboil *shirataki* in boiling water for 2 minutes. Cut into 4 inch (10cm) long pieces and drain in colander. If using *harusame,* parboil it in boiling water for 3 minutes, or soak in boiling water for 15 minutes. Drain and cut into 4 inch (10cm) long pieces.

10. Cut leeks diagonally into ½ inch (1cm) thick slices, holding the knife at about a 45° angle to length of leek.

11. Arrange all ingredients attractively on large platter with serving chopsticks or fork, and place on the table.

Cooking and Serving

1. Bring chicken and broth to boil, then put equal amounts of each ingredient into the pot from the platter. Do not put all ingredients into the pot at once. When things in the pot are done, each person serves himself from the pot, dipping the food into the dipping sauce before eating. Small amounts of condiments, as desired, are put into the sauces and eaten along with food.

2. As diners eat what is in the pot, additional amounts should be put in so that the pot always contains equal amounts of each ingredient.

Notes: If you are not able to cook this dish at the table because you do not have the necessary utensils, select a casserole dish with a size that corresponds to the number of diners and cook the ingredients in it in the kitchen. When done, serve at the table. If cooking one time is not enough, repeat 2 to 3 times, or as necessary.

When all items have been eaten from the pot, add precooked *udon* (Japanese wheat noodles) or cooked rice to the tasty broth left over in the pot. Add a little soy sauce, boil a short while, and eat.

Preparation time: 30 minutes

Ingredients

7 ounces (200g) chicken, boned but skin left on

7 ounces (200g) lean pork, thigh or loin, sliced thin

7 ounces (200g) fish (codfish, sea bream, sea bass, salmon), filleted

4 clams or other shellfish in shell

8 large shrimp

1 block *tofu*

8 *shiitake* **or other fresh mushrooms**

7 ounces (200g) devil's tongue jelly noodles (*shirataki***) or 1 ounce (25g) Chinese bean thread noodles (***harusame***)**

4 ounces (100g) carrot

4 leaves Chinese cabbage

1 to 2 leeks

4 large scallops or 6 ounces (150g) raw oysters, shucked

Ponzu **sauce: ½ cup lemon juice or commercial ponzu*, ½ cup soy sauce, ½ cup water**

Broth: 5 cups *dashi* **(page 26) or water, 2 tablespoons soy sauce, 2 tablespoons** *mirin,* **2 tablespoons** *sake* **or dry white wine, ½ teaspoon salt**

Condiments

About 4 inch (10cm) thick section long white radish (*daikon***), peeled and grated, then mixed with a couple dashes ground red pepper (1½ tablespoons per serving)**

½ tender long scallion, sliced paper-thin crosswise (½ tablespoon per serving)

---

*Has a citric flavor

Meat, Seafood and Vegetables Cooked in an Earthenware Container

This is a one-pot meal in which all kinds of delicacies of land and sea are cooked in a clear broth. You need not prepare all ingredients. Choose about 8 kinds, but be sure to prepare one kind of meat, 2 kinds of seafood, *tofu*, mushrooms, *shirataki,* Chinese cabbage and leek.

Preparation

1. Mix ingredients for *ponzu* sauce, and prepare condiments.

2. Cut chicken, meat and fish into 1½ inch (4cm) squares. Soak clams in salt water and keep in a dark, cool place until cooking time to remove sand. Rinse under running water just before using. If using oysters, put into colander, immerse in salt water (1 teaspoon salt per cup water) and rinse by shaking colander in the water.

3. Peel shrimp, but leave tails and very last section of each shell nearest the tail attached. Remove veins by inserting toothpick under each vein at the center of back and pulling up gently. The vein should come up neatly in one piece.

4. Cut *tofu* into 1 inch (2.5cm) cubes and drain.

5. Remove stems from mushrooms. If desired, carve out a criss-cross design on top for decoration. If using another type of mush-room, use as is.

6. Parboil *shirataki* in boiling water for 2 minutes. Cut into 4 inch (10cm) long pieces and drain in colander. If using *harusame,* par-boil it in boiling water for 3 minutes, or soak in boiling water for 15 minutes. Drain, and cut into 4 inch (10cm) long pieces.

7. Cut carrot crosswise into ¼ inch (0.5cm) thick rounds.

8. Cut Chinese cabbage leaves into 2 inch (5cm) squares.

9. Cut leeks diagonally into ½ inch (1cm) thick slices, holding the knife at about a 45° angle to length of leek.

Cooking and Serving

1. In the kitchen, arrange equal amounts of each ingredient attrac-tively in your empty serving pot until the container is full. Do not put in all ingredients at nce. Put remaining ingredients on a platter with serving chopsticks or fork, and place on dining table.

2. At the kitchen stove, bring broth to boil in another pot, pout it over ingredients in the serving pot until the broth is just below the level of the ingredients, and heat the pot until broth simmers, then carry it to the heating apparatus on the dining table for cooking.

3. When ingredients are done, each person serves himself from the pot, dipping the cooked food into the sauce before eating. Small amounts of condiments, as desired, are put into the sauce and eaten along with the food.

4. Additional ingredients should be put into the pot so that the pot always contains equal amounts of each ingredient. If the level of soup falls too low, add extra hot broth.

Note: If you are not able to cook this dish at the table because you do not have the necessary utensils, select a casserole dish with a size that corresponds to the num-ber of diners and cook the ingredients in it in the kitchen. When done, serve at the table. If cooking one time is not enough, repeat 2 to 3 times, or as necessary.

Meat, Seafood and Vegetables Cooked on a Grill

CALORIES	650
PROTEIN	43.1g
FATS	34.6g
CARBOHYDRATES	43.7g

Condiments
If various types of condiments are prepared, not only will the different changes in flavor throughout the meal be enjoyable for diners, but also the colorings of the condiments will help liven up the table. Shown in the photograph above (from top left clockwise) are mustard, grated long white radish, lemon, seven-flavored cayenne and scallion.

How to Make Sesame Seed Sauce
Grind the seeds while still hot and fragrant. The key point is to grind them fully until the oil comes out.

To the ground seeds, add sugar and *miso* and mix well. Add remaining seasonings and mix them all together well.

Preparation time: 30 minutes

Ingredients
1¼ pounds (550g) boneless meat
  (beef, pork, chicken, lamb, liver),
  2 to 3 kinds according to your
  taste
8 large or medium shrimp
4 littleneck clams
2 leeks
1 to 2 onions
4 ounces (100g) carrot
8 *shiitake* or other fresh
  mushrooms
1 to 2 sweet or white potatoes
4 green peppers
2 small, thin eggplants, about 3
  ounces each
1 to 2 ears corn, shucked
2 tablespoons vegetable oil

Sesame seed sauce: 4
  tablespoons white sesame
  seeds, 1 tablespoon *miso*, 1
  tablespoon sugar, 2 tablespoons
  mirin, 2 tablespoons rice vinegar
  or slightly diluted cider vinegar,
  2 tablespoons *sake* or dry white
  wine, 4 tablespoons soy sauce, 1
  teaspoon prepared Japanese
  mustard
Ponzu sauce: ½ cup lemon juice
  or commercial *ponzu**, ½ cup
  soy sauce, ½ cup water

Condiments
About 4 inch (10cm) thick section
  long white radish (*daikon*),
  peeled and grated (1½
  tablespoons per serving)
½ tender long scallion, sliced
  paper-thin crosswise (½
  tablespoon per serving)
4 wedges lemon
Seven-flavored cayenne (*shichimi
  togarashi*)
Prepared mustard

Utensil
Electric iron grill or skillet

---

*Has a citric flavor

Meat, Seafood and Vegetables Cooked on a Grill

Frying on an iron grill is a popular way of cooking, but the Japanese style of eating the food with a soy sauce-based sauce adds a new twist. Dieters should choose low-calorie ingredients such as seafood, and avoid those which require much oil for frying, such as eggplant.

Preparation
1. Prepare dipping sauces. For sesame sauce, first toast seeds in a dry frying pan without oil over medium-to-high heat, shaking pan constantly from the beginning to prevent burning. When popping begins, transfer to a grinder or earthenware mortar, and grind until smooth with pestle while the seeds are still hot. Add all other ingredients for the sauce to the ground seeds, and mix well. For *ponzu* sauce, mix all ingredients together.
2. Prepare 2 to 3 condiments of your choice.
3. Cut meat into squares.
4. Peel shrimp, but leave tails and very last section of each shell nearest the tail attached. Remove veins by inserting toothpick under vein at center of back and pulling up gently. The vein should come out neatly in one piece.
5. Soak clams in salt water and keep in a dark, cool place until cooking time to remove sand. Rinse under running water just before using.
6. Cut leeks crosswise into 2 inch (5cm) lengths.
7. Peel onions and slice crosswise into ¼ inch (0.5cm) thick round pieces. Stick toothpick through each slice to prevent rings from separating.
8. Cut carrot crosswise into thick rounds, and parboil in boiling water containing a pinch of salt until half done.
9. Remove stems from mushrooms.
10. Cut potatoes crosswise into thin rounds.
11. Halve green peppers lengthwise. Remove seeds and ribs. If pieces are large, halve again.
12. Slice eggplants into thin rounds. Soak in water 5 minutes to prevent discoloring.
13. Cut corn crosswise into thick rounds and parboil in boiling water containing a pinch of salt until half done.
14. Arrange all ingredients attractively on large platter with serving chopsticks or fork.

Cooking and Serving
1. Heat iron grill on dining table; heat oil and grill equal amounts of ingredients. When food is done, each person mixes condiments into dipping sauce, then serves himself from the grill, dipping food into the sauce and condiments before eating.
2. As everyone eats what is on the grill, additional amounts should be added so that the grill always has equal amounts of each ingredient on it.

Note: You can also fry foods deliciously without using oil. Vegetables, however, will dry out, and should be wrapped in aluminum foil first before placing on grill. This will also keep the flavor from escaping.

MEAT DISHES

In Japanese cooking of olden times, meat dishes centered on chicken, but duck and quail were also used. In modern times, however, with the Westernization of eating habits, pork and beef also appear in the daily diet.

The characteristic feature of Japanese meat dishes is the use of Japanese-style flavorings such as soy sauce, *miso* (fermented soybean paste), *sake* (rice wine), *mirin* (sweet rice wine for cooking), and so on. The methods of cooking are designed to bring out the natural flavor of the meat and to produce a finished dish which is not oily or heavy. The cooked-meat smell, unpleasant to many Japanese, is subdued also by the addition of seasonings. Since the amount of oil does not exceed what is absolutely necessary, the number of calories is held down.

Chicken: Chicken used in Japan is almost exclusively of the broiler type. Therefore, tender meat with a light taste is most ideally suited for Japanese dishes. Chicken contains a lot of high-quality protein, is generally low in fat and is easy to digest.

Pork: Since pork is less expensive than beef, it is used often in Japan, as is chicken, in daily household cooking. It is served not only in Japanese-style dishes but in Western- and Chinese-style dishes as well. Therefore, the volume and frequency of pork consumption is higher than that for all other meats. Since pork is extremely rich in vitamin B—containing nine to ten times as much as in beef and chicken, although the protein content is about the same—it is an excellent source of nutrition.

Beef: Raising of beef cattle in Japan is geared toward production of marbled meat, called *shimofuri*, because it commands a very high price in the market. Because there are lines of fat running throughout marbled meat, it is very tender and highly prized as a "high-class" meat. The fat content, however, is higher and therefore marbled meat should be used sparingly by a dieter.

Skewered Chicken
(yakitori)

CALORIES 336
PROTEIN 25.9g
FATS. 13.5g
CARBOHYDRATES 17.0g

Rolled Chicken Stuffed with Scallions

CALORIES 316
PROTEIN 18.8g
FATS. 17.9g
CARBOHYDRATES 10.8g

Deep-fried Marinated Chicken

CALORIES 345
PROTEIN 18.2g
FATS. 24.1g
CARBOHYDRATES 11.8g

Preparation time: 40 minutes

Ingredients
10 ounces (300g) chicken, boned, skin left on
7 ounces (200g) chicken livers
4 *shiitake* or other fresh mushrooms
4 green peppers
1 to 2 leeks
2 tablespoons vegetable oil (if using frying pan)
Seven-flavored cayenne (*shichimi togarashi*)

Yakitori sauce: 2 tablespoons sugar, ½ cup *mirin*, 1 cup soy sauce, 1 cup *sake* or dry white wine

Utensils
20 to 30 fine metal or bamboo skewers, about 5 inches (12cm) long

Skewered Chicken *(yakitori)*

This dish has a very delicious flavor and, if served at parties, your guests will certainly be delighted. The calorie data is for grilling. If a frying pan is used, the number of calories per person will be approximately 60 more.

Preparation

1. Combine seasonings for *yakitori* sauce and simmer in open pot over medium-to-high heat for 20 to 30 minutes, or until volume decreases by one-third. Put into tall glass.
2. Cut chicken into 1 inch (2.5cm) squares.
3. Cut liver into approximately 1 inch (2.5cm) squares. Soak in water for 5 minutes to remove blood. Drain.
4. Remove stems from mushrooms. Cut top in half or quarter. If small, use whole.
5. Quarter green peppers lengthwise. Remove seeds and ribs, then cut each quarter again crosswise into halves or thirds.
6. Cut leeks into 1 inch (2.5cm) lengths.
7. If using bamboo skewers, soak in water for several minutes to prevent them from burning during use.
8. Thread 4 to 5 pieces of chicken onto skewers, leaving a little space between each piece to allow even cooking. Thread some skewers with liver and others with vegetables, or alternate pieces of chicken and leek.

Putting *yakitori* sauce in tall glass makes it easier to dip skewered items.

Cooking

1. It is preferable to grill *yakitori* on a barbecue rack over charcoal. If not available, an oven broiler or stove-top grill can be used. If none of the above is available, a frying pan can be substituted. If using oven broiler, broil skewered chicken and liver for a few seconds only or until lightly browned. Pull out, dip into or brush with *yakitori* sauce, and broil again, turning skewers over. Repeat 2 to 3 times the procedure of coating with sauce, grilling and turning over. Do not cook until dry.
If using outdoor grill, barbecue or stove-top grill with rack and pan below, keep heat at medium to high, and follow procedure outlined above. During grilling, much of the fat between skin and meat will drop down.
If using frying pan, heat 1 teaspoon vegetable oil and sauté skewered chicken and liver 2 to 3 minutes, or until half-done, turning over several times. Coat meat with *yakitori* sauce and sauté. Repeat 1 or 2 times more until done. Because sugar and soy sauce will burn easily, you will have to wash the frying pan after each batch to prevent burning. Repeat this procedure until meat and liver are all done, about 2 times more.
2. To cook skewered vegetables, follow coating and grilling procedure for meat, or grill without sauce. If not using sauce, sprinkle with salt immediately after cooking and a squeeze of lemon, if desired.

Serving

Serve *yakitori* on large platter immediately after grilling. At the table, sprinkle with *shichimi togarashi,* if desired.

Cooking time: 40 minutes, plus 20
minutes for marinating chicken

Ingredients
4 chicken thighs, or about 14
  ounces (400g) thigh meat,
  boned, skin left on
4 long scallions
Cornstarch or potato starch for
  dusting chicken
1 tablespoon vegetable oil
½ cup *sake* or dry white wine
1 leek

Marinade: 2 tablespoons sugar, ½
  teaspoon salt, 2 tablespoons
  soy sauce, 2 tablespoons *sake*
  or dry white wine, 1 teaspoon
  ginger juice

Cooking time: 20 minutes, plus 20
minutes for marinating chicken

Ingredients
14 ounces (400g) chicken, boned,
  skin left on
Cornstarch or potato starch for
  coating meat
About 3 cups vegetable oil for
  deep-frying
4 green peppers

Marinade: 2 tablespoons soy
  sauce, 1 tablespoon *sake* or dry
  white wine, 1 teaspoon ginger
  juice

Rolled Chicken Stuffed with Scallions

Scallions are rolled up inside boned chicken thighs. The rolls are then sautéed in *sake* and sweetly flavored with soy sauce and sugar. By tying up the rolls with string beforehand, you can produce a neat product.

Preparation
1. Stretch out chicken into oblong shape. Pierce skin with fork here and there so marinade will seep in. Score meat side where thick to make it of even thickness all over. Marinate for 20 minutes, turning occasionally.
2. Cut scallions crosswise into same length as the chicken.
3. Drain chicken and put on chopboard skin side down. Sift cornstarch thinly over meat and scallions. Put 3 to 4 pieces of scallion in center of meat and roll up. Wind roll with string along its length, leaving ½ inch (1cm) space between each wind.
4. Cut leek crosswise into 2 inch (5cm) sections, then each section again in half lengthwise. Finally, cut each half lengthwise into needle-fine strips, soak in water for a few minutes, and drain.

Cooking
1. Heat frying pan or heavy sauce pan with oil over high heat. Put in chicken rolls and sauté along seam first to seal it, then sauté rest until rolls are slightly browned all the way around, or for about 5 minutes, turning over occasionally with tongs. Drain off excess oil.
2. To the pot add ½ cup *sake* or dry white wine and cook about 7 minutes over medium-to-low heat, then add remaining marinade to the pan. Cook over low heat for 7 to 8 minutes with tight lid on. While cooking, rolls should be turned over occasionally.

Serving
Cut rolls into 1 inch (2.5cm) thick rounds after they are cooked, and serve with remaining sauce and the needle-fine cut leek.

Deep-fried Marinated Chicken

Chicken is preflavored to give it more body. It is then dusted with starch and deep-fried until reddish-brown. Deep-fried foods are high in calories but satisfying, therefore, even dieters should occasionally eat some. Choose low-calorie side dishes.

Preparation
1. Cut chicken into 1½ inch (4cm) squares.
2. Marinate chicken for 20 minutes, turning over occasionally.
3. Cut green peppers in half, and remove seeds and ribs.
4. Toss chicken lightly in cornstarch, and shake off excess.

Cooking and Serving
1. Heat oil to 320°F (160°C) in a Chinese *wok* over high heat. Fry green peppers for only 30 seconds and drain.
2. Slide chicken into oil, 4 to 5 pieces per batch, and fry 3 to 4 minutes, or until golden brown, turning over occasionally.
3. Serve chicken hot with green peppers.

Chicken Meat Balls

CALORIES 212
PROTEIN 15.0g
FATS. 12.9g
CARBOHYDRATES 5.8g

Boiled Chicken and Long White Radish Flavored with Wine

CALORIES 277
PROTEIN 18.2g
FATS. 31.7g
CARBOHYDRATES 9.5g

Sautéed
Thin Ground-chicken Loaf

CALORIES 276
PROTEIN 19.0g
FATS. 19.7g
CARBOHYDRATES 2.4g

Cooking time: 25 minutes

Ingredients
10 ounces (300g) ground chicken
2 cups *dashi* (page 26) or
   homemade chicken stock (no
   seasonings added)
2 teaspoons sugar
1 tablespoon *sake* or dry white
   wine
1½ tablespoons soy sauce
1 tablespoon *mirin*
4 ounces (100g) green beans
4 teaspoons salt

To season chicken: 1 teaspoon
   sugar, 2 teaspoons soy sauce, ½
   egg, 2 tablespoons cornstarch
   or potato starch

Chicken Meat Balls

Here meat balls made of ground chicken are cooked with a mild flavoring in a fish stock to which sugar, *sake* and soy sauce have been added. Thus the balls are tender and juicy. Because there is little broth, bring it to a boil over medium heat, then reduce heat to low.

Preparation and Cooking
1. Combine ground chicken with its seasonings, and mix thoroughly until it forms a paste.
2. Simmer *dashi* with sugar, *sake*, soy sauce, and *mirin*. Scoop a handful of meat mixture onto your palm. Form a circle with the thumb and index finger of that hand, and squeeze the meat mixture through the circle into golfball-sized balls. Scoop the ball with a spoon, adjust the shape, and drop into the piping hot soup one after another, taking care they do not stick to one another.
3. Let the balls cook in the soup for 3 to 5 minutes, and leave in soup until ready to serve.
4. Cut off tops and bottom tips from green beans, then cut beans crosswise into 2 to 3 sections. Put into boiling water containing ¼ teaspoon salt, cook for 2 minutes, and drain. To flavor, boil again for 1 minute in soup left over from cooking chicken balls.

Serving
Serve meat balls hot or at room temperature with green beans as complement. Pour remaining soup on top, if desired.

Note: You can make a high-volume snack by boiling balls together with long white radish. Cut radish into desired size and boil in water until half-done. While boiling radish, cook meat balls as shown in steps 2 and 3, but remove from broth when done. Transfer radish to broth for meat balls and boil until tender. Put balls back and cook through. With this variation, it is necessary to double the quantity of the original broth.

Cooking time: 40 minutes

Ingredients
7 ounces (200g) long white radish
   (*daikon*)
14 ounces (400g) chicken, boned,
   skin left on or removed
1½ cups water
1½ teaspoons sugar
2 tablespoons *mirin*
Pinch of salt
1½ tablespoons soy sauce
3 tablespoons red wine

Boiled Chicken and Long White Radish Flavored with Wine

This is a simple and casual boiled dish, but when a small amount of wine is added, its faint acidic taste and aroma add just the right touch to give the final dish a fancy flavor. The wine should be added only at the last or its flavor will be lost.

Preparation
1. Cut long white radish into 1 inch (2.5cm), irregularly shaped pieces, cut at oblique angles to each other.
2. Cut chicken into 2 inch (5cm) squares.

Cooking and Serving
1. Bring 1½ cups water to boil over medium heat. Put in chicken and radish and boil about 15 minutes.
2. Season with sugar, *mirin*, salt, and soy sauce in that order. Boil 10 minutes more, or until tender.
3. Last, add red wine and boil 1 to 2 minutes more.
4. Serve hot in individual bowls.

Sautéed Thin Ground-chicken Loaf

This is a Japanese-style thin meat loaf with an interesting soy sauce-ginger flavor. If fatty meat is used, the loaf will shrink when cooked. Thus, fairly lean chicken is recommended. We tell you here how to cook a large loaf quickly using a frying pan.

Cooking time: 30 minutes

Ingredients
2 inches (5cm) leek
14 ounces (400g) ground chicken
2 teaspoons vegetable oil
2 teaspoons toasted white sesame
 or poppy seeds
4 sprigs watercress

To season chicken: 2 teaspoons
 sugar, 2 teaspoons soy sauce,
 2 teaspoons *sake* or dry white
 wine, 1 teaspoon ginger juice,
 ½ beaten egg

Preparation
1. Mince leek fine.
2. Mix ground chicken, seasonings for meat and leek until smooth.

Cooking and Serving
1. Heat small frying pan or small shallow saucepan with oil for 1 minute over medium-to-low heat. Put in meat mixture and spread evenly until ½ inch (1cm) thick all over, then smooth the surface with a spatula. Sauté 3 to 4 minutes, or until slightly browned, taking care not to burn it. Turn it over carefully. If too difficult to turn, cut into 4 portions and turn over one by one.
2. Just after turning over, sprinkle with sesame seeds or poppy seeds while the surface is still hot or the seeds will not stick to the meat.
3. Continue to sauté 2 to 3 minutes more, or until well done. When meat has almost cooled, cut into triangular, oblong or fan-shaped pieces.
4. Serve at room temperature with watercress.
Note: You can savor a different kind of delicious flavor by using 1 tablespoon of *miso* in lieu of the 2 teaspoons of soy sauce in the seasoning for the chicken. It is satisfactory also to use the oven instead of a frying pan to cook this dish.

Sautéed Ground Beef–Tofu Hamburgers

This is a soy sauce-flavored hamburger which combines ground beef with *tofu*. These small-sized burgers are tasty, soft and pleasing to the palate and can be enjoyed by young and old alike. For a variation, you may want to substitute ground pork.

Cooking time: 30 minutes

Ingredients
1 block *tofu*
½ leek or 1 long scallion
½ inch (1cm) cube fresh ginger
10 ounces (300g) ground beef
1 egg, stirred
3 tablespoons flour
Lettuce, watercress, boiled
 spinach, or French-fried
 potatoes
1 tablespoon vegetable oil
Prepared mustard

To season meat: ⅓ teaspoon salt,
 1½ tablespoons soy sauce

Preparation
1. Cut *tofu* into 3 to 4 portions, cover with dry cheesecloth and press with both hands to remove excess water. Change the cheesecloth for another dry one or wrap again in paper towels. Let stand 10 minutes to drain, then mash coarsely with fork.
2. Mince leek or scallion and ginger.
3. Cover hand with plastic bag, and using that hand, mix ground beef, seasonings, *tofu,* leek, ginger, stirred egg, and flour. Divide mixture into 8 portions and make into tiny oval-shaped or round patties.
4. Prepare greens or potatoes for complement.

Cooking
Heat 1 tablespoon oil in frying pan, and sauté meat patties over medium heat until both sides are light brown, or about 4 to 5 minutes per side.

Serving
Serve hot with mustard.

Beef, Potatoes and Onions Cooked with Flavorings

CALORIES 317
PROTEIN 20.5g
FATS. 8.9g
CARBOHYDRATES 35.1g

Grilled Rare Beef with Condiments

CALORIES 179
PROTEIN 22.4g
FATS. 7.8g
CARBOHYDRATES 3.6g

Rolled Beef
with Vegetables

CALORIES 214
PROTEIN 18.7g
FATS. 7.9g
CARBOHYDRATES 14.1g

Sift cornstarch lightly over the upper part only so vegetables will adhere better to meat.

Wrap meat around vegetables. Fix last wrap with toothpick so they will not come apart when cooked.

Sauté rolls in the pan, add broth and, coating rolls with sauce, heat through.

Cooking time: 40 minutes

Ingredients
10 ounces (300g) beef, thinly
    sliced
1 pound (500g) white potatoes
    (about 3 to 4 medium)
2 onions
4 teaspoons vegetable oil
⅔ cup water
¼ cup *sake* or dry white wine
2 tablespoons sugar
3 tablespoons soy sauce

Beef, Potatoes and Onions Cooked with Flavorings

This dish has a down-home flavor reminiscent of mother's cooking. The potatoes are flavored with the delicious taste of the beef. Extremely popular because of its hearty flavor, this item will disappear quickly from the table.

Preparation
1. Cut beef into 1½ inch (4cm) long pieces.
2. Peel potatoes and cut into quarters, or smaller pieces if the potato is extra large. Soak in water for 5 minutes.
3. Peel onions and cut in half lengthwise. Put each half cut-side down and slice into thin, half-moon-shaped slices of equal thickness.

Cooking and Serving
1. Heat thick-bottomed pot with 2 teaspoons oil, and sauté beef until color turns, or about 2 minutes. Take out and set aside.
2. Add 2 teaspoons oil to the pot. Sauté onions and potatoes about 2 minutes, stirring until they are well-coated with oil.
3. Put in ⅔ cup water, *sake* or dry white wine and sugar. Boil until potatoes are half done, then add soy sauce. Put beef back into the pot, and continue to boil until potatoes are tender, or about 15 minutes.
4. Serve hot in individual bowls.

Cooking time: 40 minutes

Ingredients
14 ounces (400g) beef, rump or
    tenderloin, in a 2 inch (5cm)
    thick block
1 teaspoon vegetable oil

Condiments
7 ounces (200g) long white radish
    (*daikon*), roughly a 4 inch (10cm)
    thick section
½ tender long scallion (green part
    only)
½ lemon
4 teaspoons soy sauce (1 per
    serving)

Grilled Rare Beef with Condiments

The distinctive flavors of grated radish, scallion green, and lemon and the taste of soy sauce go very well with beef. You can savor fully the delicious flavor of the beef with only180 calories per person. You may prefer to cut the finished beef into thin slices instead of cubes.

Preparation
1. Remove any fat from beef. Cut into 3 equal portions against the grain.
2. Prepare condiments. Grate white radish. If too watery, drain off excess liquid, but do not squeeze to remove.
3. Cut scallion green crosswise into thin rounds. Slice lemon or cut into wedges.

Cooking and Serving
1. Brush beef with oil, then grill on both sides under broiler for just a few minutes, or only until surface color turns light brown.
2. Cool beef on a wire rack, and cut into 1 inch (2.5cm) cubes.
3. Put beef on individual plates, garnish with grated white radish, then sprinkle with sliced scallion green. At the dining table, sprinkle about 1 teaspoon of soy sauce over each serving of beef. Mix it in lightly with the grated radish and scallion, then squeeze lemon on top.

Preparation time: 40 minutes

Ingredients
4 ounces (100g) carrot
4 ounces (100g) burdock root
1 teaspoon vinegar
2¼ cups water
1 teaspoon sugar
1 teaspoon soy sauce
4 ounces (100g) green beans
¼ teaspoon salt
**10 ounces (300g) lean beef or
    pork, thinly sliced**
**Cornstarch or potato starch for
    dusting meat**
1 tablespoon vegetable oil
4 sprigs watercress

**Broth: ¼ cup water, 1 tablespoon
    sugar, 1 tablespoon *sake* or dry
    white wine, 1 tablespoon *mirin*, 3
    tablespoons soy sauce**

Rolled Beef with Vegetables

This is a meat dish in which colorful vegetables such as carrot, green beans and burdock root are wrapped inside slices of beef. Although served cool, the rolls are delicious and easy to eat. Why not try them for a party?

Preparation
1. Scrape carrot and cut lengthwise into strips about 6 inches (15cm) long and roughly ¼ inch (0.5cm) square.
2. Scrape the thin, brown skin off burdock root with the back of a knife, and cut crosswise, then lengthwise, into strips of the same size as carrot. Soak in water containing 1 teaspoon vinegar for 5 minutes immediately after cutting to prevent discoloring. Drain and rinse off vinegar.
3. Bring to boil ¼ cup water containing 1 teaspoon each of sugar and soy sauce, add carrot and burdock root, and boil until done, or about 5 minutes.
4. Cut off tips from green beans and remove strings. Bring 2 cups water containing ¼ teaspoon salt to a boil, and parboil beans in pot without lid until tender, or about 3 minutes, and drain. Cool quickly under running water and drain.
5. Cut beef slices into 2 inch (5cm) wide strips. The length will vary according to the size of your slices.
6. Spread beef on chopboard and sift cornstarch lightly over the upturned part only.
7. Make several bunches of vegetables using 2 pieces each of burdock root, carrot strips and green beans.
8. Put one bunch of vegetables on the dusted side of each slice of beef and roll as shown in the pictures (page 51). Fix last wrap with toothpick so they will not come apart when cooked. Make several rolls. Dust outside of each lightly with cornstarch or potato starch.

Cooking
1. Heat pan with 1 tablespoon vegetable oil over high heat, and sauté beef rolls until slightly browned all over, turning over occasionally.
2. Add broth. When it begins to simmer, reduce heat to low, and continue to sauté about 5 minutes, turning rolls over continuously until well flavored and well coated with sauce, then turn off heat.

Serving
After the rolls have cooled slightly, cut each crosswise into 1 to 2 inch (2.5 to 5cm) thick rounds. Serve several pieces on each person's plate, and pour remaining sauce on top. Watercress makes a good garnish for these rolls.

Advice for Weight-watchers
When meat is used in solid pieces, such as steak or pork chops, it can be served simply. For the calorie-conscious, however, cooking skillfully with thinly sliced meat will make it possible to eat delicious dishes with a feeling of satisfaction, even if the quantity of meat is small. The key point is that to the eye thinly sliced meat has more volume than whole pieces and will provide more volume when combined with vegetables.
In Japanese cooking, there are many dishes calling for thinly sliced meat. In Japan, thinly sliced meat is sold in various degrees of thickness and usually cut according to the particular use to which it will be put.

Sautéed Pork with Ginger

CALORIES 401
PROTEIN 18.3g
FATS. 32.3g
CARBOHYDRATES 4.9g

Boiled Pork with Japanese-style Sauce

CALORIES 308
PROTEIN 31.5g
FATS. 10.4g
CARBOHYDRATES 19.7g

Sautéed Pork with Ginger

This "speed dish" is made by flavoring thinly sliced pork with fresh ginger and soy sauce, then frying it quickly. Chinese cabbage or onions used in lieu of cabbage are also very good. The trick to making this delicious dish is to cook it very quickly at high temperature.

Cooking time: 15 minutes

Ingredients
14 ounces (400g) pork, thinly sliced
3 teaspoons ginger juice
2 to 3 leaves green cabbage
2 tablespoons vegetable oil

Marinade: 1 teaspoon sugar, 1 tablespoon *sake* or dry white wine, 3 tablespoons soy sauce

Preparation
1. Cut pork into 2 inch (5cm) long pieces. Mix 1 teaspoon ginger juice with marinade ingredients and marinate pork for 10 minutes, turning over occasionally.
2. Remove hard center sections of cabbage, and cut leaves into small squares.

Cooking and Serving
1. Heat frying pan well with 1 tablespoon oil over high heat, and sauté pork until half-done, or about 3 minutes, stirring from the beginning to prevent pieces from sticking together. Push pork to one side of the pan.
2. Add 1 tablespoon oil to the pan again, put in cabbage and sauté 1 to 2 minutes, then stir in pork. Pour on any remaining marinade and 2 teaspoons ginger juice, stir quickly and turn off heat.
3. Serve hot on individual plates.

Cooking time: 1 hour

Ingredients
1¼ pounds (550g) boneless pork, in 1 piece
½ leek
4 slices fresh ginger
4 white potatoes
3 carrots
4 ounces (100g) green beans
¼ teaspoon salt

Mustard sauce: 2 tablespoons soy sauce, 1 teaspoon prepared Japanese mustard
Sesame seed sauce: 2 tablespoons white sesame seeds*, 3 tablespoons *miso*, 1 tablespoon sugar, 2 teaspoons rice vinegar or slightly diluted cider vinegar, 5 tablespoons soup from boiling pork

*Toast sesame seeds in frying pan without oil over medium-to-high heat, shaking pan constantly from the beginning to prevent burning. When popping begins, transfer to a grinder or earthenware mortar, and grind until smooth while seeds are still hot.

Boiled Pork with Japanese-style Sauce

This recipe calls for vegetables being boiled together with the meat, but raw vegetables can be served instead. The pork is good also when eaten with grated radish and a vinegar-soy sauce dipping sauce. Weight-watchers will want to use lean meat.

Preparation and Cooking
1. Wrap pork with string, leaving a small space between each wind.
2. Cut leek crosswise into 1 inch (2.5cm) lengths.
3. Bring to boil about 5 cups water or enough to cover pork. Put in meat, leek and ginger, and boil about 30 minutes over medium heat.
4. While pork is boiling, prepare other ingredients.
a) Peel potatoes and cut in half or quarter.
b) Peel carrots and cut crosswise into 2 inch (5cm) lengths, then lengthwise into about 1 inch (2.5cm) wide, oblong pieces.
c) Cut off tops and bottom tips from green beans and remove strings. Cut beans crosswise into 2 to 3 pieces.
d) Mix ingredients for mustard sauce and/or sesame seed sauce.
5. When the pork is almost done, add potatoes and carrots. If the level of soup is too low, add some boiling water. Cook until everything is tender. To test pork, stick the thickest part through with a fine skewer. If it can be stuck through easily, the meat is done. Cooking time will be 40 to 50 minutes in all.
6. Bring to boil 2 cups water containing ¼ teaspoon salt. Put in green beans and cook without lid for 3 minutes, or until tender. Drain and cool quickly under running water.

Serving
Cut pork into ¼ inch (0.5cm) thick pieces, and serve with the vegetables. Dip meat into dipping sauce of your choice before eating.

SEAFOOD DISHES

Japan is among the world's top consumers of seafood. As a consequence, the number of fish dishes in Japanese cooking is large, and the varieties of methods for preparing fish and shellfish in season are extremely numerous.

Representative of seafood dishes is *sashimi,* extremely fresh, high-quality fish dressed to be eaten raw. The techniques of preparing *sashimi*, which were developed to their highest level of artistry in Japan, present the diner with an opportunity to appreciate the flavor of fish and shellfish to the fullest degree. Like *sashimi,* the grilling of fish and shellfish over direct flame also holds a central place in Japanese seafood cooking. Compared to other methods, this way of cooking at high temperature helps to lock in the flavor and juices of the ingredients and protect their nutritional content. Moreover, in browning and singeing the surface, a delightful grilled flavor and savory aroma are created, and one can relish fully the taste of the fish.

In addition to the above methods of preparation, seafood is also served in one pot dishes cooked at the table; boiled at low-to-medium temperature in a small amount of liquid with seasonings so the flavorings will be absorbed; steamed, taking advantage of the natural flavor of the fish, to produce a dish with light flavor; deep-fried to create a heavy rich flavor and sense of volume; served in Japanese-style salads, and in many other ways— the method of preparation appropriate to the kind of seafood being used.

It should be stressed again that fish dishes have many healthy features. Compared to meat dishes, they are lower in calories, easier to digest, provide good-quality protein, and contain high levels of calcium. Moreover, the oil in fish works to lower the body's cholesterol level and raises the efficiency of the adult body in warding off disease.

Grilled Salmon with Teriyaki Sauce

CALORIES 223
PROTEIN 21.5g
FATS 11.4g
CARBOHYDRATES 4.4g

Grilled Scallops with Teriyaki Sauce

CALORIES 183
PROTEIN 23.5g
FATS 5.2g
CARBOHYDRATES 7.6g

Fish Baked in Aluminum Foil with Vegetables

CALORIES 99
PROTEIN 16.5g
FATS. 0.5g
CARBOHYDRATES 5.3g

Grilled Salmon with Teriyaki Sauce

Fish such as salmon, tuna, and yellowtail are delicious with *teriyaki* sauce. They can be grilled, but we tell you here how to cook them simply in a frying pan. Grated radish goes well as a condiment and also aids in the digestion of oily fried foods.

Cooking time: 15 minutes, plus 10 minutes for marinating

Ingredients
**4 small salmon steaks, or use yellowtail, tuna, or halibut
2 inch (5cm) thick section long white radish (*daikon*)
1 tablespoon vegetable oil (if using frying pan)
4 sprigs watercress**

Teriyaki **sauce: 1 teaspoon sugar, 2 teaspoons** *sake* **or dry white wine, 1 tablespoon** *mirin,* **2 tablespoons soy sauce**

Preparation
1. Mix ingredients for *teriyaki* sauce thoroughly until sugar dissolves.
2. Marinate fish in sauce for 10 minutes, turning over occasionally. Drain before cooking.
3. Peel white radish and grate. Drain but do not press out water.

Cooking and Serving
1. If grilling fish, grill as is. If frying, heat frying pan well with oil over medium heat, and sauté for 2 to 3 minutes, or until slightly browned. Turn fish over gently, taking care not to break them up. Sauté 2 minutes more, then drain off excess oil.
2. Add *teriyaki* sauce left over from marinating, and cook until fish are well coated, or for 1 to 2 minutes.
3. Serve salmon hot, with watercress and grated white radish at the side. If desired, pour on top of salmon the sauce remaining from the frying.

Cooking time: 10 minutes, plus 10 minutes for marinating

Ingredients
**8 large or 12 medium sea scallops (2 to 3 per serving)
8 spears asparagus
¼ teaspoon salt
1 tablespoon vegetable oil (if using frying pan)**

Teriyaki **sauce: 1 teaspoon sugar, 2 teaspoons** *sake* **or dry white wine, 1 tablespoon** *mirin,* **2 tablespoons soy sauce**

Grilled Scallops with Teriyaki Sauce

This is an adaptation of salmon *teriyaki.* Protect the natural flavor of the scallops by cooking them for only a short time. If you cook them on high heat only until both sides turn burnt umber, they will be juicy and savory.

Preparation
1. Mix ingredients for *teriyaki* sauce thoroughly until sugar dissolves.
2. Marinate scallops in sauce for 10 minutes, turning over occasionally. Drain before cooking.
3. Cut asparagus in half crosswise. Heat water to boil with ¼ teaspoon salt. Boil hard sections first for 2 minutes, then add top sections and boil 2 minutes more. Cool under running water immediately to prevent color from fading.

Cooking and Serving
1. If grilling scallops, grill as is. If frying, heat frying pan well with oil over medium heat, put in scallops, and sauté about 2 minutes. Turn over and sauté 1 minute more, or until slightly browned and cooked through. Cooking time will depend on size.
2. Add *teriyaki* sauce left over from marinating, and cook until scallops are well-coated, or about 1 minute.
3. Serve scallops with asparagus beside them as complement. If desired, pour on top of scallops the sauce remaining from the frying.

Cooking time: 40 minutes

Ingredients
4 fillets of white-fleshed fish (cod, flounder, sea bass)
1 teaspoon salt
4 teaspoons *sake* or dry white wine
2 ounces (50g) carrot
2 green peppers
1 onion
4 *shiitake* or other fresh mushrooms
½ lemon, cut into 4 wedges or sliced

Cooking time: 30 minutes

Ingredients
4 fillets of white-fleshed fish (cod, flounder, sea bass)
4 *shiitake* or other fresh mushrooms
4 ounces (100g) fresh spinach
1 block *tofu*
½ teaspoon salt
4 tablespoons *sake* or dry white wine

Ponzu sauce: 4 tablespoons lemon juice or commercial *ponzu**, 4 tablespoons soy sauce, 4 tablespoons water

Condiments
About 4 inch (10cm) thick section long white radish (*daikon*), peeled and grated (1½ tablespoons per serving)
½ tender long scallion, sliced paper-thin (½ tablespoon per serving)

*Has a citric flavor

Fish Baked in Aluminum Foil with Vegetables

This method of cooking without oil, freely combining ingredients and adding flavor just before eating, is the most ideal for dieters. Its deliciousness depends upon choice of fish and vegetables, so you should choose items of the highest quality and freshness.

Preparation
1. Preheat oven to 320°F (160°C).
2. Remove skin and bones from fish, if any, and sprinkle each fish with a pinch of salt and 1 teaspoon *sake* or dry white wine, and let stand for 10 minutes.
3. Slice carrot crosswise into thin rounds then, if desired, carve the rounds into flower shapes.
4. Seed green peppers, then slice crosswise into thin rings.
5. Peel onion and slice crosswise into thin rounds.
6. Remove stems from mushrooms.
7. Moisten centers of 4 sheets of aluminum foil 10 inches (25cm) square slightly with *sake* to prevent fish from sticking to the foil, then put on fish and other ingredients, arranging them attractively, and sprinkle with a pinch of salt.
8. Bring the two sides of the foil together above the center of the ingredients, and seal by folding down twice in consecutive ½ inch folds and then securing both right and left edges in the same way.

Cooking and Serving
1. Bake in oven for about 15 minutes.
2. Serve hot on individual plates with wedges or slices of lemon.

Variation
Baked Fish Flavored with Sake

White-fleshed fish flavored with *sake* (rice wine) is baked in gratin dishes together with *tofu,* fresh mushrooms and spinach. It is then eaten in a refreshing Japanese style with a citric-flavored sauce.

Preparation
1. Preheat oven to 425°F (220°C).
2. Remove skin and bones from fish, if any, and cut meat into about 1½ inch (4cm) square pieces.
3. Remove stems from mushrooms.
4. Bring pan of water to boil, add a pinch of salt and cook spinach about 2 minutes and drain. Cool under running water, gently squeeze out excess water, and cut into 1½ inch (4cm) lengths.
5. Cut *tofu* into 1 inch (2.5cm) cubes and drain.
6. Divide all solid ingredients, except condiments, into 4 portions and put each attractively into individually sized gratin dishes or other ovenproof bakeware.
7. On top of the fish, *tofu* and vegetables in each container, sprinkle a little salt and 1 tablespoon *sake* and put on lid. If lid is not available, use aluminum foil on top.

Cooking and Serving
1. Bake 15 to 20 minutes.
2. Eat hot with raw condiments and *ponzu* sauce.

Tempura

CALORIES 669
PROTEIN 25.2g
FATS. 38.8g
CARBOHYDRATES 49.8g

Ingredients for Basic Batter
Combine 1 egg, enough cold water to make a little more than 1 cup liquid (egg included), and 1 cup sifted light flour.

How to Make Batter
Mix egg in bowl. Add water and stir. Then, add all the flour and mix lightly. Do not blend until smooth.

Coating with Batter (shrimp)
Holding shrimp by tail, dip in batter up to the shell segment nearest the tail. Do not dip tail.

How to Fry (shrimp)
Holding shrimp by tail, let it slide down the side of the pan into the oil. Wait one second, then release tail.

Cooking time: 80 minutes

Ingredients
4 small, very thin white-fleshed fish (smelts or sardines), cleaned and opened flat
4 ounces (100g) mixed vegetables (carrots, green peas, and corn), frozen
4 large or 8 medium shrimp
1 small squid
½ sweet potato
4 ounces (100g) winter squash, peeled and seeded
½ onion
4 ounces (100g) carrot
2 ounces (50g) green beans
4 *shiitake* or other fresh mushrooms
1 long scallion
About 4 cups vegetable oil for deep-frying*
Small amount of flour for dusting

Batter: 1 egg, enough cold water to make a little more than 1 cup liquid (egg included), 1 cup sifted light flour
Dipping sauce: 1 cup *dashi* (page 26), 3 tablespoons *mirin,* 4½ tablespoons soy sauce

Condiments
6 tablespoons (about 4 inch (10cm) thick section) peeled and grated long white radish (*daikon*) (1½ tablespoons per serving)
2 teaspoons peeled and grated fresh ginger (½ teaspoon per serving)
4 wedges lemon
4 dashes salt (optional)

Utensils
A deep-fryer, thick steel pot, Chinese *wok,* or deep-frying pan

---

*Always fry *tempura* with previously unused oil so the color of your *tempura* will be good and the items light.

Tempura

The ingredients for *tempura* are coated and deep-fried until crisp, using a superb cooking method which protects their freshness and nutritional content. By grasping just a few essentials, you too can make delicious *tempura* simply at home.

Preparation

1. Refrigerate all ingredients for batter ahead of time, but do not combine. If left at room temperature, batter will become gluey and the fried food will be too oily and heavy.

2. Prepare fish and vegetables for frying.

a) Defrost frozen mixed vegetables.

b) Peel shrimp, but leave each tail and just the last section of shell nearest each tail attached. Next, prepare as shown in photographs on right.

c) If using fresh squid, separate the soft plastic-like backbone and head from body with fingers, and pull tentacles and viscera out of the body along with backbone. Cut off crosswise the triangular tail section, including fins. Rinse and peel down the very fine tissue-like skin, scraping from head to tail. Cut crosswise into ½ inch (1cm) wide rings, or cut open lengthwise, then into small oblong pieces. Make several short cuts all around the edges to prevent curling when cooked.

Remove veins by inserting toothpick under vein at center of the back and pulling up gently.

Make 3 short cuts across the stomach to prevent curling when cooked.

d) Cut sweet potato crosswise, if large in diameter, into ¼ inch (0.5cm) thick rounds. If small, cut diagonally into oval slices. Soak in water for 5 minutes to prevent discoloring, and drain.

e) Cut squash into small oblong pieces or into comb shapes, following curve of squash.

f) Peel onion and cut in half from top to bottom. Put each half cut-side down and cut into semicircular pieces. Stick toothpick through each to prevent rings from separating.

g) Peel carrot and julienne into 2 inch (5cm) long fine strips.

h) Cut green beans into 2 inch (5cm) lengths.

i) Remove stems from mushrooms.

j) Cut scallion into 1 inch (2.5cm) lengths.

3. To make dipping sauce, add *dashi, mirin,* and soy sauce to pan and heat. When ingredients begin to boil, turn off heat.

4. Prepare condiments.

5. Begin heating up oil in Chinese *wok* over high heat to around 320°F (160°C).

6. While oil is heating, prepare batter. First, stir 1 egg with chopsticks or whisk, but do not beat. Add enough water to make a little more than 1 cup of liquid, and mix well with chopsticks. Put in sifted flour all at one time, and mix with chopsticks. If it gets lumpy, do not be concerned. Do not overmix, and do not place near stove or other hot place or it will become gluey. Refer to the step-by-step photographs on page 63.

7. Pat dry fish, shrimp and squid, as well as defrosted mixed vegetables.

Cooking

1. Test whether the heating oil is hot enough by dropping a bit of batter from chopsticks into the oil. If it sinks close to the bottom then comes up, the oil is not ready yet; if it sinks half-way then comes up, the temperature is around 320°F (160°C) and suitable for frying hard vegetables. Begin with hard ingredients which require longer cooking time at low temperature, such as potatoes, then move to tender vegetables, fish, shrimp and squid which need a higher temperature of 340 ~ 360°F (170 ~ 180°C).

2. To cook sweet potato, squash, and onion, dip first in batter, then slide gently into the oil, 5 to 6 pieces per batch. Separate them from one another and turn over. Fry for about 3 minutes or until done, turning over occasionally, then drain.

3. To cook mushrooms, coat only the underside of the tops with batter by letting them float on the batter and by putting additional batter onto uncoated spots with a spoon. Fry about 1 minute and remove.

4. Put green beans on a large flat plate. Dust finely with dry flour, then divide beans into clusters of 3 to 4 pieces each. Ladle over enough batter to lightly cover beans and mix a little. Using chopsticks or slotted ladle, slide the clusters into the oil one by one, and fry for about 2 minutes, taking care they do not come apart.

5. Repeat the above procedure for carrots, making clusters of the same size as beans, but with twice as many pieces of carrot.

6. Repeat the same procedure for frozen mixed vegetables, but instead of making clusters, cover items with batter, mix, then scoop up 1 to 2 tablespoons of mixture with a slotted ladle, and slide into the oil. When in, quickly round and flatten them using chopsticks or fork. When they become a little crispy, turn them over. Fry for about 3 minutes in all.

7. Combine small shrimp and scallion, then coat and deep-fry as in step 6.

8. Add a little more new oil to the *wok* and wait until the oil gets hotter than before for the fish and shrimp—to around 360°F (180°C).

9. Dust fish, shrimp, and squid thinly with dry flour, dip in batter, holding tails with fingers, and slide into the oil with skin side of the fish up. For shrimp and squid, either side will do. Fry fish for about 3 minutes, shrimp 4 minutes (depending on the size) and squid 1 minute. Refer to the step-by-step photographs on page 63.

Serving

1. After ingredients are cooked, serve as quickly as possible, putting equal amounts on individual plates, or all on a large platter, with absorbent paper underneath.

2. Put about 1½ tablespoons grated white radish in the right-hand corner of the plate or on a small side plate and, using fingers, top radish with ½ teaspoon grated ginger so it looks like a snow-capped mountain.

3. Warm dipping sauce and put into small individual bowls. At the dining table, diners should mix small amounts of grated white radish and ginger into the sauce, and dip the fried food into it before eating. A squeeze of lemon and salt can be substituted for the dipping sauce, if desired.

Deep-fried Sardines Marinated in Vinegary Sauce

CALORIES 384
PROTEIN 23.3g
FATS. 22.4g
CARBOHYDRATES 19.2g

Salmon-Tofu Balls

CALORIES 316
PROTEIN 27.4g
FATS. 21.2g
CARBOHYDRATES 11.0g

Cooking time: 70 minutes

Ingredients
½ **onion**
1 **ounce (25g) carrot**
2 **to 3 green peppers**
½ **lemon**
2 **dried red chilies**
8 **medium sardines or smelts,**
    about 4 to 6 inches (10 to 15cm)
    long
Flour for coating fish
About 3 cups vegetable oil for
    deep-frying

Deep-fried Sardines Marinated in Vinegary Sauce

This dish, which has a delightful piquant sauce, can be made well in advance. It can also be eaten just 1 to 2 hours after fixing but is most delicious when held overnight. The addition of soy sauce adds a Japanese touch to this European dish.

Preparation

1. Mix all ingredients for marinade thoroughly until sugar and salt dissolve.
2. Slice onion from top to bottom into paper-thin rounds and carrot paper-thin crosswise.
3. Seed green peppers, then slice into thin rounds. Slice lemon thinly.
4. Cut off just the tips of the tops of dried red peppers. Insert a chopstick into the pepper, and twist the chopstick to separate seeds from the pod. Pull the chopstick out and rub the pod between your fingers, and the seeds will drop out of the pod. Cut crosswise into 3 pieces.
5. Marinate vegetables along with red pepper.
6. Prepare fish. If small, remove scales and gut, but leave head and tail attached (the head can be removed after frying, if desired). Clean under running water and pat dry with dry dish towel or paper towel. If fish are big, cut off heads and slice meat away from central bone, first along one side of the bone, from head to tail, then turning fish over, slice meat off along other side and discard bone.
7. Coat fish thinly but thoroughly with flour, especially on the inside, to prevent splattering when fried. Dust off excess flour.

Cooking

1. Heat about 3 cups of vegetable oil to 320°F (160°C) in a Chinese *wok*, deep-fryer or heavy steel pot over high heat. Slide fish into oil, fry until golden brown, or about 6 to 7 minutes, turning over occasionally. The cooking time is relatively longer than for ordinary deep-frying because the bones of the fish must be soft enough to eat.*
2. Drain on absorbent paper or on a wire rack over shallow drain pan. At this stage, you can remove heads of small fish, if desired. (If the head is removed at the beginning, it is difficult to protect the shape of the tender fish, and they may open at the stomach.)
3. Marinate fish immediately after frying while they are still very hot.** Let stand for 40 to 60 minutes, turning over occasionally. Longer marinating will make the fish more tender and tasty. They can be refrigerated for 1 to 2 days.

Serving

Serve fish at room temperature with marinated vegetables on top and around sides. Garnish with sliced lemon.

*If you deep-fry using the following method, even large fish with heads attached will cook all the way through and the head and bones will be edible. First, fry the fish slowly on low heat, or about 320°F (160°C), so that the heat penetrates the center, then remove fish. After all the fish have been fried this way, raise the temperature of the oil to high, put in fish again and fry for a short time.

**If the fish are put into the marinade immediately after they come out of the oil, the flavor of the marinade will seep into them more easily.

Salmon-Tofu Balls

In this recipe we call for eating these bite-sized balls piping hot with grated ginger and soy sauce, but as they are lightly salted already, you may prefer to eat them plain or with a refreshing squeeze of lemon.

Cooking time: 40 minutes

Ingredients
Pinch of salt
Dash of *sake* or dry white wine
2 fillets of salmon, about 10
   ounces (300g)
1 block *tofu*
Flour
About 3 cups vegetable oil for
   deep-frying
4 leaves leaf lettuce
4 teaspoons soy sauce (1 per
   serving)
2 teaspoons peeled and grated
   fresh ginger (½ teaspoon per
   serving) or 1 teaspoon prepared
   Japanese mustard

Preparation
1. Heat small amount of water containing a pinch of salt and a dash of *sake* (rice wine) or dry white wine, cook salmon in it for 2 to 3 minutes and drain. Remove skin and bones, if any, and flake fish meat with fingers. Grind in earthenware mortar with pestle until coarsely mashed, or chop fine on chopboard.
2. Cut *tofu* into 6 to 8 portions, and boil in boiling water for 2 minutes to remove excess moisture. Drain in cheesecloth-lined colander. When drained, wring edges of the cloth to remove remaining excess moisture.
3. Add *tofu* to the salmon, put in 2 tablespoons flour, season with ⅔ teaspoon salt, and mix until pasty. Form this into small balls about the size of a walnut, and cover thinly and evenly with flour.

Cooking
1. Heat about 3 cups of vegetable oil to 320°F (160°C) in a Chinese *wok*, deep-fryer or heavy steel pot over high heat.
2. Slide several balls into the oil one by one. Turn them over right away and continue to fry until golden brown, or for 3 to 4 minutes, turning over occasionally. Cook any remaining balls in the same way.
3. Drain on absorbent paper or on a wire rack over a shallow drain pan.

Serving
Serve hot on lettuce leaves. Eat with soy sauce and grated ginger or prepared mustard.

Japanese-style Snacks Using Canned Fish

Canned fish packed in water or oil is convenient to have on hand because it can be flavored and used in many kinds of dishes. If you keep various kinds of fish in stock, you can whip up quick snacks to serve with drinks such as *sake* and beer when guests suddenly drop by.

Sardines Packed in Oil with Flavor Added, Japanese-style
Squeeze the oil out of the sardines and pile fish on a plate. Serve with grated long white radish (or radish grated and mixed with a couple dashes of powdered hot red pepper) and chopped scallions as condiment. Sprinkle a little soy sauce on top.
Tuna Mixed with Soy Sauce and Mustard
To coarsely broken up tuna, add chopped scallions and minced ginger and mix lightly. Pile in bowl. Immediately before eating, mix with soy sauce-mustard dressing made by mixing together 2 tablespoons rice vinegar or slightly diluted cider vinegar, 3 tablespoons soy sauce and ½ teaspoon prepared mustard (Japanese or other type without vinegar or spices).
Miniature Fried Mackerel Cakes
Coarsely break up 7 ounces (200g) canned mackerel packed in water. Add 1 teaspoon ginger juice (grated fresh ginger and squeeze), ½ beaten egg, 3 tablespons flour, 1 teaspoon soy sauce, and 2 tablespoons chopped scallions and mix. Heat 1 tablespoon vegetable oil in frying pan. Add mackerel one tablespoon at a time and flatten into smooth even cakes. Fry until nicely brown in color. Serve hot.

Salad of Crab and Wakame with Vinegar Dressing

CALORIES 701
PROTEIN 9.9g
FATS 0.9g
CARBOHYDRATES 5.5g

Salad of Tuna and Wakame with Soy Sauce Dressing

CALORIES 249
PROTEIN 41.6g
FATS 19.8g
CARBOHYDRATES 19.1g

Salad of Hard-shelled Clams with Miso Dressing

```
CALORIES . . . . . . . . . . .  521
PROTEIN . . . . . . . . . . . . . 4.5g
FATS. . . . . . . . . . . . . . . . 0.5g
CARBOHYDRATES . . . . . 8.0g
```

How to Prepare *Wakame*

Dried *wakame* is pictured on the left and fresh *wakame* (preserved in salt) is shown on the right.

Soak in water until big and tender, about 10 minutes for dried *wakame* and 2 to 3 minutes for fresh. Do not oversoak.

Drain off water, put into fresh boiling water and cook about 10 seconds. Drain again.

If center vein is hard, cut it out. Cut *wakame* into the same sized pieces as the other items in the dish.

Cooking time: 20 minutes

Ingredients
2 ounces (50g) fresh *wakame*
  (seaweed) or ⅕ ounce (5g) dried
7 ounces (200g) crab meat,
  canned or parboiled fresh
1 small cucumber, about 3 ounces
  (80g)
½ teaspoon salt
4 leaves leaf lettuce

Vinegar dressing: 5 tablespoons
  rice vinegar or slightly diluted
  cider vinegar, 4 teaspoons
  sugar, ⅔ teaspoon soy sauce, ⅓
  teaspoon salt

Salad of Crab and Wakame with Vinegar Dressing

The fresh colors of this salad and its sweet-sour dressing stimulate the appetite and will set off your whole menu to advantage. At only 70 calories per person, this item is a must for the weight-watcher's repertory of diet dishes.

Preparation and Cooking

1. Rinse fresh *wakame* to remove salt, and soak in water for 2 to 3 minutes. If using dried *wakame,* soak in water for 10 minutes until swollen and tender. Drain off water, put into fresh boiling water and cook about 10 seconds. Drain again and cut into 1 inch (2.5cm) lengths. If center vein is still hard, cut it out.
2. Mix ingredients for vinegar dressing.
3. Remove bones from canned crab. If using boiled crab in its shell, remove the meat. Break crab meat coarsely with fingers, and pre-flavor with 1 teaspoon rice vinegar.
4. Rub cucumber between the hands with ½ teaspoon salt to tenderize it and to remove excess water, then wash off salt, and slice paper-thin crosswise.
5. Just before serving, mix all ingredients, and season with vinegar dressing.

Serving

Line small deep bowls with one leaf of lettuce each, mound in crab mixture, and serve right away. If desired, top with a pinch of ginger which has been cut into needle-fine strips.

Cooking time: 20 minutes

Ingredients
4 ounces (100g) fresh *wakame*
  (seaweed) or ⅓ ounce (10g)
  dried
10 ounces (300g) canned tuna
1 teaspoon lemon juice
1 small cucumber, about 3 ounces
  (80g)
½ teaspoon salt
1 to 2 tomatoes

Soy sauce dressing: 2
  tablespoons soy sauce, 3
  tablespoons rice vinegar or
  slightly diluted cider vinegar,
  ½ tablespoon sesame oil or
  vegetable oil

Salad of Tuna and Wakame with Soy Sauce Dressing

This salad, which calls for *wakame* and lots of canned tuna, is high in volume. *Wakame* is a noncaloric health food rich in calcium and phosphorus. Weight-watchers should drain the oil well from the tuna before using.

Preparation and Cooking

1. Rinse fresh *wakame* to remove salt, and soak in water for 2 to 3 minutes. If using dried *wakame,* soak in water for 10 minutes until swollen and tender. Drain off water, put into fresh boiling water and cook about 10 seconds. Drain again and cut into 1 inch (2.5cm) lengths. If center vein is still hard, cut it out.
2. Mix ingredients for soy sauce dressing.
3. Break tuna coarsely and season with 1 teaspoon lemon juice.
4. Rub cucumber between the hands with ½ teaspoon salt to tenderize it and to remove excess water, then wash off salt, and slice paper-thin crosswise.
5. Cut tomatoes into small cubes.
6. Just before serving, mix all ingredients and season with soy sauce dressing.

Serving
Mound into small deep bowls and serve right away.

Cooking time: 25 minutes

Ingredients
3 ounces (80g) hard-shelled
  clams, such as cherrystones or
  littlenecks
½ teaspoon *sake*
4 long scallions
Japanese green horseradish
  (*wasabi*)

Miso dressing: 2 tablespoons
  white (sweet) *miso*, 2
  tablespoons rice vinegar or
  slightly diluted cider vinegar, 1
  tablespoon *sake* or dry white
  wine, 1 tablespoon sugar; or 2
  tablespoons ordinary light *miso*
  for soup, 2 tablespoons rice
  vinegar or slightly diluted cider
  vinegar, 1 tablespoon sugar, 1
  tablespoon *mirin*

Salad of Hard-shelled Clams with Miso Dressing

In this recipe, the taste of the scallions goes very well with the flavor of fresh clams. Add to these a *miso* dressing and you have a fancy seafood dish. If *wakame* is added, you can enjoy yet another taste treat.

Preparation
1. Mix all ingredients for *miso* dressing thoroughly until sugar dissolves.
2. If clams are fresh enough to eat raw, put into colander, immerse in water containing 1 teaspoon salt per cup of water, shake colander gently in the water, then drain. If the clams need cooking, cook as explained below. If using fresh raw tuna, cut into 1 inch (2.5cm) cubes.

Cooking
1. Bring to boil a small amount of water containing ½ teaspoon *sake* or dry white wine, and parboil clams for only 1 minute, or until cooked through. Drain. Do not overcook or they will shrink and become tough.
2. Cut long green onions into 1 inch (2.5cm) lengths. Bring to boil a small amount of water containing a pinch of salt, put in white and tougher green parts of onions first and boil 1 minute, then put in tender green parts and boil 1 minute longer. Drain and cool.
3. Just before serving, combine all ingredients and mix with *miso* dressing.

Serving
Mound dressed food in small bowls and serve with pinch of *wasabi* on top, if desired. For an alternate way of serving, combine all ingredients and mound in individual bowls, then pour on about 2 tablespoons dressing, and top with *wasabi,* if desired. Diners can mix the ingredients with the dressing at the dining table, using their own chopsticks or forks.

Seaweed as Healthy Low-Calorie Food

Seaweed is a storehouse of minerals and vitamins, including calcium, phosphorus and vitamin A. Although the body cannot digest it, it contains a lot of dietary fiber which contributes to efficient movement of food in the digestive tract and is said to help lower the amount of cholesterol in the body.

In addition to being an excellent health food, seaweed contains no calories. Thus, everyone should consider introducing it into the diet.

In Japan, as you no doubt know, many kinds of seaweed are used in cooking, with *nori* (dried laver), *konbu* (kelp) and *wakame* being the main items. *Nori* is very lightly toasted and eaten as is and, of course, used in *sushi*. *Konbu* is an essential ingredient for *dashi* (soup stock), is used in lightly boiled and seasoned dishes, and so on. *Wakame* is an ingredient for soups or, when very briefly boiled, finds use in salads. Since *wakame* has no strong odor or taste, its use in Western cooking is by all means recommended. Try it in soups and salads. It goes very well with French dressing and mayonnaise. When a little soy sauce is added to the dressing, it will make it even more delicious. If added to your seafood salad, *wakame's* vibrant green color will make the dish beautiful and will, no doubt, perk up appetites.

Varieties of Sashimi

Sashimi is a typical dish in Japanese cookery. It is probably correct to say that this style of preparation and eating preserves to the maximum degree the original flavor of the fish.

When making fish into *sashimi*, the most important problem is freshness of items used. As long as they are of the freshest quality and good enough to consume raw, almost any fish can be used. Ideally, one should use ingredients which are in season or at their peak of flavor. If these two points are observed, the proper conditions exist for making delicious *sashimi*.

The style of serving *sashimi* is also very important. It is not simply lined up on a serving utensil. Rather, it is necessary to dispense it in a way that is aesthetically pleasing and that makes it look delicious. Long white radish cut into long spaghetti-fine filaments or various seasonal vegetables or seaweed are added as garnishes, and *wasabi* (Japanese green horse-radish) or grated fresh ginger are provided as condiments. These garnishes and condiments enhance the beauty and taste of the *sashimi* and add a look of freshness and elegance. Moreover, they help provide nutritional balance, effectively aid in digestion, and remove any bad taste from the mouth after eating. The condiments add aroma and hot flavoring, help to weaken the fishy smell of the raw fish, and greatly enhance the taste of the *sashimi*. For dipping sauce, soy sauce is indispensable.

Below we introduce several of the fish typically used for *sashimi*.

Sashimi of tuna, halibut, squid and a variety of yellowtail

Above are 4 variations of ways to serve *sashimi* including the universally popular tuna. The method of serving which makes the best use of the empty space of the plate—serving a balanced variety of *sashimi* and adding embellishments which improve coloring—is the beauty of Japanese cooking.

a. Tuna

We illustrate here various methods of cutting tuna. You will note that cutting is done in a way that the product will please the eye. Tuna's oily pink portion, called "toro," has good body and is popular with connoisseurs while the red portion has a simple refreshing taste.

b. Halibut

The compact meat of this white-fleshed fish is sliced off thinly. It makes a light *sashimi* with a firm texture which is pleasantly chewable.

c. Squid

This fish makes a beautiful white *sashimi*. One can best appreciate squid's characteristic firm consistency by eating it raw. One attractive way of serving it is in pinwheel shapes rolled with *nori* (dried laver).

d. Yellowtail

Yellowtail is a first-class fish when used for *sashimi*. It is light in taste.

Marinated mackerel

Mackerel is a typical common-class fish in Japan. When eaten as *sashimi*, it is first sprinkled with an ample amount of salt and left to stand for several hours to remove its excess moisture. The meat is then marinated in vinegar to remove its strong oily and fishy smell. Although regarded as a fish consumed by the common people, when prepared in this fashion, it is quite delicious.

Sashimi of sea bream and turbo

Spring is the season for serving *sashimi* of sea bream and turbo, a typical mollusk in Japan. Garnishing with rape blossoms to add color evokes a feeling of spring.

a. Sea bream

Because the shape, color, and flavor of this fish are good, sea bream is prized highly in Japan as the "king of fish" and is not to be omitted at the table on festive occasions. It is best eaten as *sashimi* if one wishes to fully savor its firm texture and light flavor. Because of its high quality, sea bream is high-priced.

b. Turbo

This mollusk has a pleasantly chewable texture and unique taste. When preparing turbo or any other shellfish for use as *sashimi,* one should keep them alive until time for preparation.

Tataki of bonito

The skin of this fish is oily, but delicious. When making bonito into *tataki,* the skin side only is grilled very quickly over direct flame until singed, usually not more than one minute. This method makes the otherwise hard skin part easy to eat, while the inside remains uncooked and tender. It is then immersed in ice water which gives the skin a frosty appearance. It is served, as shown in the photograph, with a lot of condiments such as sliced garlic and scallions along with *ponzu* sauce (page 33).

Sashimi of balloon fish

Sashimi made with balloon fish is light and has a unique and exceedingly delicate taste on the tongue. It is generally sliced so thinly that it is transparent and then is laid out beautifully on a plate. The skin is also delicious and is often served with the fish. Because the balloon fish contains a very strong poisonous substance in parts of its body, such as the liver and ovaries, it can be served in Japan only in those restaurants specialized in its preparation.

75

Common Japanese Fish and Shellfish

The varieties of fish and shellfish available to Japanese cooks will differ, of course, from what is available here. The following are some of their common types, easily substituted with the species given.

Aji (horse mackerel): The varieties of *aji* are extremely numerous. It is used for *tataki* (a type of *sashimi*), or is salted and grilled, or spread open and deep-fried. You can substitute smelts, sardines, or whitebait.

Asari (short-necked clams): These bivalves have egg-shaped shells about 1½ inches (4cm) long and many speckles on their ash-colored shell surfaces. When shelled, they are used in dishes such as *nuta* (a side dish of shellfish, *wakame,* and scallions with vinegared *miso*), *zosui* (a porridge of rice and vegetables, and *nabemono* (one-pot table cooking). You can substitute littleneck or cherrystone hard-shelled clams.

Buri (yellowtail): These are very good salted, coated with *teriyaki* sauce and grilled or boiled with flavorings. The young fish (called *hamachi*) is extremely delicious as *sashimi*. The North American yellowtail is a silver perch, somewhat different fish but can be substituted. Other fish to substitute are mullet, mackerel, silverside, and carp.

Ebi (shrimp or prawns): There are many varieties, and whatever variety is used, you'll enjoy its full flavor best eaten as *tempura.*

Hamaguri (clams): A clam is said to indicate the harmony of husband and wife because the pattern on both sides of the shell is the same and the two sections of the shell adhere to each other nicely, making a perfect pair. Clams, therefore, are often served on festive occasions such as weddings. These clams are used for soups and best substituted by chowder clams or quahogs.

Hotategai (scallops): One side of the shell is white and bulges out rather far. The other side of this fan-shaped bivalve is purple-red in color. When very fresh, they are used for *sashimi,* but can be grilled with *teriyaki* sauce. They are also tasty when deep-fried or sautéed. In the United States, scallops are almost always sold shucked (out of the shell).

Ika (squid): The one most commonly eaten in Japan is the *surume-ika.* There are many cooking methods ranging from *sashimi* to boiling, grilling, sautéing, and deep-frying. When preparing, it is necessary to avoid overcooking or it will become tough. Squid is also processed in dried form and is sometimes salted or pickled.

Katsuo (bonito): The flavor is rich and the skin portion, in particular, has a good taste. The oil content is low. It is delicious made into *tataki* (a type of *sashimi*) but can also be boiled or grilled with *teriyaki* sauce.

Kisu (sillago): A graceful fish, its meat is white and soft. A regular ingredient for tempura, it is also salted and grilled or cooked in broth-based dishes. Substitute whitefish or trout.

Maguro (tuna): Fresh tuna is grilled or boiled, but its most general use is for *sashimi.* Also, tuna is hardly ever omitted as an ingredient for *sushi.* The value of the cut depends on the part of the fish from which it comes. The part valued most highly is the section around the stomach called *toro,* which contains a lot of oil. The red lean portion is low in fat and has a simple refreshing taste.

Saba (mackerel): This spoils very quickly, so one should make sure it is fresh. Its taste is rich, and its meat oily. This fish has a good flavor when boiled or grilled, but is especially delicious boiled with *miso* paste and fresh ginger, which kills its fishy smell. It is tasty also when heavily salted, then marinated in vinegar (called *shime-saba*).

Sake (salmon): Because salmon has a delicious flavor, the whole fish, from head to tail, can be put to many uses, such as grilling or cooking stock-based dishes. Additionally, the eggs, which are pickled in salt, are prized very highly. These are called *ikura* (or *sujiko*) and are used for hand-formed or hand-rolled *sushi.*

Tai (sea bream): There are many varieties. Referred to as "the fish that doesn't spoil," its flavor does not diminish quickly like that of most fish, and it has no peculiarities. It can be used diversely such as for *sashimi,* in stock-based dishes, or can be grilled.

VEGETABLE DISHES

In Japanese cooking, vegetable dishes play the dual roles of enhancing the beauty of the main dish and evoking a feeling of the season at the table.

Japan has a temperate climate with four distinct seasons, and there are a rich variety of vegetables associated with each season. Consequently, it is very basic to Japanese cooking to use very fresh vegetables when they are at their season's peak and to prepare them in a way that will bring to life the flavors which they hold. It is not sufficient that the vegetables just be delicious. They must also be superior in nutrition and beautiful to the eye.

Vegetables contain an abundance of fiber which, despite the fact it cannot be digested and absorbed by the body as nutritive substance, is especially efficacious in promoting healthy functioning of the lower intestinal tract.

Vegetables, especially soybeans, are also storehouses of vitamins and minerals. Vitamins and minerals play a key role in bodily processes, and an inadequacy of them in the diet can become the cause of various imbalances in the body. We all should aim to take in an abundant quantity of fresh vegetables on a daily basis to protect and preserve our health.

To capitalize on the good features of vegetables, good cooking methods such as quick treatment (e.g., draining and flavoring) and short, rapid cooking are necessary to prevent them from losing their nutrients as well as their flavor and natural color.

People eating low-calorie food in order to lose weight are apt to feel unsatisfied if the quantity of food consumed in their meal is small in volume. Adding a lot of vegetables will make a meal high in volume, and eaters will come away from the table feeling full. Another added bonus is that the menu can be greatly diversified by changing and playing up the selection of vegetables.

Japanese-style Salads

Salad of Bean Sprouts with Soy Sauce Dressing

CALORIES. 92
PROTEIN. 2.9g
FATS 6.6g
CARBOHYDRATES 5.6g

Salad of Bean Sprouts with Vinegar Dressing

CALORIES. 48
PROTEIN. 4.5g
FATS 1.4g
CARBOHYDRATES 4.5g

Quickly Pickled Vegetables

CALORIES. 63
PROTEIN. 2.0g
FATS 0.2g
CARBOHYDRATES 11.5g

Boiled Spinach with Sesame Seed Dressing

CALORIES. 53
PROTEIN. 3.9g
FATS 2.5g
CARBOHYDRATES 5.0g

Salad of Asparagus and Chicken with Mustard Dressing

CALORIES. 43
PROTEIN. 7.4g
FATS 0.2g
CARBOHYDRATES 3.7g

Long White Radish and Carrot Marinated in Vinegary Sauce

CALORIES. 39
PROTEIN. 0.6g
FATS 0.1g
CARBOHYDRATES 8.4g

Japanese-style Salads

Here you are introduced to six new exciting taste treats in salads. In them, soy sauce and the fragrance of sesame seeds, the pungent taste of mustard, and vinegar's acidity all help to bring out the natural flavor of the vegetables.

Cooking time: 20 minutes
Ingredients
7 ounces (200g) bean sprouts
4 ounces (100g) carrot
3 green peppers

Soy sauce dressing: 1 tablespoon vegetable oil, 1 tablespoon sesame oil, 3 tablespoons soy sauce, 2 tablespoons rice vinegar or slightly diluted cider vinegar

Cooking time: 20 minutes
Ingredients
7 ounces (200g) bean sprouts
3 ounces (80g) cucumber
2 ounces (50g) ham
½ inch (1cm) cube fresh ginger
2 teaspoons toasted sesame seeds

Vinegar dressing: 2 teaspoons sugar, 3 tablespoons rice vinegar or slightly diluted cider vinegar, 1½ tablespoons soy sauce

Preparation time: 10 minutes, plus half-day for pickling
Ingredients
2 leaves green cabbage
6 ounces (150g) cucumber
1 stalk celery
2 ounces (50g) carrot
½ onion
1 inch (2.5cm) cube fresh ginger

Pickling ingredients: 2½ teaspoons salt, ½ cup rice vinegar or slightly diluted cider vinegar, 1 tablespoon *sake* or dry white wine, 1 tablespoon *mirin*, ¼ cup water

Salad of Bean Sprouts with Soy Sauce Dressing

1. Mix ingredients for dressing.
2. Wash bean sprouts under running water and drain.
3. Cut carrot into 1 inch (2.5cm) long fine strips.
4. Quarter green peppers lengthwise and remove seeds and ribs. Next, slice each quarter crosswise into long fine strips.
5. Bring to boil 3 cups water containing ¼ teaspoon salt. Put in carrot and cook 1 minute, then add bean sprouts and green peppers. When water simmers again, turn off heat. Drain off water through colander, and cool quickly by fanning. Squeeze slightly to remove excess water.
6. Combine all ingredients and mix with dressing just before serving. Mound in small bowls.

Salad of Bean Sprouts with Vinegar Dressing

1. Mix ingredients for dressing.
2. Wash bean sprouts under running water and drain.
3. Cut cucumber diagonally into thin slices, then each slice into fine strips.
4. Cut ham into 1½ inch (4cm) long fine strips.
5. Bring to boil 3 cups water containing ¼ teaspoon salt. Put in bean sprouts and cook 1 minute. Drain off water through colander, and cool quickly by fanning. Squeeze slightly to remove excess water.
6. Mince ginger fine.
7. Combine all ingredients except sesame seeds and mix with dressing just before serving. Mound in small bowls, and sprinkle with toasted sesame seeds.

Quickly Pickled Vegetables

1. Mix ingredients for pickling mixture.
2. Cut cabbage leaves into 1 inch (2.5cm) squares.
3. Cut cucumber and celery into bite-sized pieces, and carrot into thin oblong pieces.
4. Slice onion thinly and cut ginger into fine strips.
5. Put all vegetables into large bowl and pour pickling mixture over them. Put a flat plate, slightly smaller than the mouth of the bowl, on top of the vegetables.
6. To press ingredients, put a weight three times that of the vegetables on top of the flat plate. The weight could be, for example, a saucepan or other container partially filled with water and slightly smaller than the bowl in diameter so the weight is evenly distributed. Leave the weight a half-day or overnight. Drain and serve.

Note: Those vegetables not used right away should be kept in the pickling mixture and refrigerated. If refrigerated, they will keep 3 to 4 days.

Cooking time: 10 minutes

Ingredients
10 ounces (300g) fresh spinach

Sesame seed dressing: 2
  tablespoons sesame seeds, ½
  teaspoon sugar, 1½ tablespoons
  soy sauce, 2 tablespoons *dashi*
  (page 26) or water

Boiled Spinach with Sesame Seed Dressing

1. To make sesame seed dressing, first toast seeds in a dry frying pan without oil over medium-to-high heat, shaking pan constantly from the beginning to prevent burning. When popping begins, transfer to dry bowl right away. Reserve about 1 teaspoon as garnish, and grind the rest while they are still hot in a grinder or in an earthenware mortar with pestle until smooth. Add all other ingredients for the dressing to the ground seeds, and mix well.

2. Bring to boil a quantity of water just sufficient to cover the spinach. When it simmers, add ¼ teaspoon salt, then put in spinach, stalk sections first, and simmer about 1 minute. Then push leafy parts into the pot, simmer 1 minute and drain. Rinse under running water, squeeze firmly but lightly and cut into 1 inch (2.5cm) long pieces.

3. Just before serving, mix spinach with sesame seed dressing and mound in small bowls. Sprinkle on top with toasted sesame seeds reserved in step 1 above.

Cooking time: 20 minutes

Ingredients
4 ounces (100g) chicken, bones,
  skin and fat removed
1 teaspoon salt
1 teaspoon *sake* or dry white wine
1 inch (2.5cm) square piece lemon
  rind
3 to 4 spears fresh asparagus

Mustard dressing: 1 tablespoon
  chicken broth, 3 tablespoons
  soy sauce, 1 tablespoon *sake* or
  dry white wine, ⅔ teaspoon
  prepared Japanese mustard.

Salad of Asparagus and Chicken with Mustard Dressing

1. Make chicken meat of even thickness all over by slicing through thick parts. Preflavor with ½ teaspoon salt and 1 teaspoon *sake* or dry white wine and let set about 10 minutes.

2. Bring to boil a small amount of water containing ¼ teaspoon salt and cook chicken for 2 to 3 minutes, or until done. Drain and retain soup (for use in dressing or other dishes). When cool, break chicken with your fingers into fine strips.

3. Cut lemon rind into fine strips.

4. Make dressing, mixing all ingredients thoroughly until mustard dissolves.

5. Bring to boil 2 to 3 cups water containing ¼ teaspoon salt and boil asparagus about 5 minutes. Drain and cool quickly by fanning. Cut into 1 inch (2.5cm) long pieces.

6. Mix chicken and asparagus with dressing just before serving. Mound in small bowls, and garnish in middle with 3 to 4 pieces of finely stripped lemon rind.

**Preparation time: 20 minutes, plus
1 hour marinating**

Ingredients
7 ounces (200g) long white radish
2 ounces (50g) carrot
1 inch (2.5cm) square piece lemon
  rind

Marinade: 2 tablespoons sugar,
  ½ teaspoon salt, ½ cup rice
  vinegar or slightly diluted cider
  vinegar, 1 tablespoon lemon
  juice

Long White Radish and Carrot Marinated in Vinegary Sauce

1. Peel long white radish and cut crosswise into 2 inch (5cm) thick blocks. Slice each block thinly down the length of the radish, then cut each slice again lengthwise into fine strips. Do the same with carrot.

2. Sprinkle long white radish strips with 1 teaspoon salt and let stand for 5 minutes. Then, wash off salt, squeeze to remove excess water, and drain in colander. Do the same with carrot.

3. Slice lemon rind thin.

4. Mix marinade and add lemon rind.

5. Squeeze white radish and carrot tightly again to remove excess water, and marinate for 1 hour, mixing occasionally.

6. Just before serving, drain slightly and mound in deep bowl.

Note: Since this dish wil keep for 2-3 days if refrigerated, you may find it convenient to make a large batch and have it ready for instant use.

Squash Boiled with Flavorings

CALORIES 127
PROTEIN 2.7g
FATS 0.3g
CARBOHYDRATES 29.8g

Vegetables and Chicken Cooked with Flavorings

CALORIES 276
PROTEIN 13.0g
FATS 14.7g
CARBOHYDRATES 24.4g

Soybeans Cooked with Sautéed Chicken Wings

CALORIES 585
PROTEIN 44.3g
FATS. 32.2g
CARBOHYDRATES 22.9g

Cooking time: 20 minutes

Ingredients
1 pound (500g) winter squash,
    such as acorn
1½ cups *dashi* (page 26) or
    canned or homemade
    chicken stock
2½ tablespoons sugar
1 tablespoon *mirin*
1½ tablespoons soy sauce

Cooking time: 1 hour

Ingredients
10 ounces (300g) chicken, boned
    and with skin left on
6 ounces (150g) carrot
6 ounces (150g) burdock root,
    fresh or canned
2 teaspoons vinegar
4 ounces (100g) lotus root, fresh
    or canned
4 dried Chinese black mushrooms
1 ounce (25g) snow peas
2 tablespoons vegetable oil

Boiling liquid: soaking water from
    mushrooms plus enough water
    to make 1½ cups liquid,
    2 tablespoons sugar,
    3 tablespoons soy sauce,
    2 tablespoons *mirin*

Squash Boiled with Flavorings

Sugar, sweet rice wine and soy sauce help to bring out the natural sweet flavor of squash. Because squash is a good yet inexpensive source of vitamins, you will want to make this into a delicious main dish, occasionally enhanced further by adding ground pork.

Preparation and Cooking and Serving
1. Cut squash in half, remove seeds and wash. Cut into 2 inch (5cm) squares. Slice off skin here and there to give surface a mottled look and to enable flavor of broth to seep in.
2. Put squash skin side down into saucepan, add *dashi,* sugar and *mirin.* Cover and boil 7 to 8 minutes over medium heat. After 4 to 5 minutes, turn pieces over gently one by one.
3. Add soy sauce and continue to boil 7 to 8 minutes more, or until tender, turning over once while boiling. Do not overcook.
4. Serve hot or at room temperature.

Vegetables and Chicken Cooked with Flavorings

Here vegetables such as carrot, burdock root and lotus root are sautéed in oil with mushrooms and chicken, then cooked with flavorings. This dish keeps well and can be refrigerated 2 to 3 days; the flavor improves with time.

Preparation
1. Cover dried mushrooms with warm water and soak 10 to 15 minutes, or until soft. Remove stems and keep soaking water.
2. Cut carrot into 1 inch (2.5cm), multi-sided, irregularly-shaped pieces.
3. Scrape brown skin off fresh burdock root with back of knife. Cut into same sized and shaped pieces as carrot. Immediately after cutting, soak in water containing 1 teaspoon vinegar for 5 minutes to prevent discoloring. Put into boiling water and cook about 3 minutes. Drain.
4. Peel lotus root, cut into ¼ inch (0.5cm) thick rounds, then soak in water containing 1 teaspoon vinegar for 5 minutes to prevent discoloring.
5. Cut chicken into 1 inch (2.5cm) squares.
6. Remove strings from snow peas. Put into boiling water with ¼ teaspoon salt, cook 2 to 3 minutes and drain.

Cooking and Serving
1. Heat a large, thick pot with 1 tablespoon oil over high heat. Put in chicken first and sauté until color changes. Then push chicken to one side of the pot and grease the rest with 1 tablespoon oil. Add vegetables, except snow peas, and sauté until everything is well-coated with oil.
2. Add liquid for boiling, plus the sugar, and boil about 5 minutes over medium heat with lid on. Add *mirin* and soy sauce and continue boiling for 20 to 25 minutes, or until everything is tender and the volume of soup has decreased by half. While the ingredients are cooking, turn them over gently.
3. Serve hot or at room temperature with snow peas on top.

Cooking time: 1½ hours, plus soaking time for beans

Ingredients
10 ounces (300g), or about 2 cups, dried soybeans
1 pound (500g) chicken wings
1 tablespoon soy sauce
1 tablespoon *sake* or dry white wine
½ leek
½ inch (1cm) cube fresh ginger
1 tablespoon vegetable oil

To season ingredients: 1 tablespoon sugar, 2 tablespoons *sake* or dry white wine, 4 tablespoons soy sauce

Soybeans Cooked with Sautéed Chicken Wings

In this country-style dish, the flavor of soy sauce permeates the soybeans, and the juice from the chicken wings helps give this dish its solid flavor. The soybeans, just by themselves, are a storehouse of good-quality vegetable protein.

Preparation
1. Rinse and soak soybeans in 6 cups water for 12 hours or overnight.
2. Just prior to cooking beans, preflavor chicken wings with 1 tablespoon each soy sauce and *sake* or dry white wine, and let stand for 20 minutes, turning over occasionally.
3. Cut leek into 1 inch (2.5cm) lengths.
4. Slice ginger thin.

Cooking
1. Leave beans in their soaking water and bring to boil over high heat. When water bubbles up, add ½ cup cold water. This helps to break down hard-to-cook substances in the beans, thus speeding up cooking time. Repeat this procedure 2 to 3 times.
2. After that, reduce heat to medium-low and continue to boil for about 1 hour, or until beans are tender. Cooking time will depend on hardness of beans.
3. While boiling, the soup should cover the beans. If the water level falls, add enough boiling water to cover beans again. Never add cold water.
4. Bubbles or scum should be skimmed occasionally with spoon.
5. While beans are being cooked, heat another thick pot with 1 tablespoon vegetable oil. When well heated, sauté ginger for ½ minute, then put in chicken wings, and sauté until slightly browned. Last, put in pieces of leek and sauté 2 minutes longer, then turn off heat.
6. After the soybeans have become tender, add them, along with their soup, into the pot containing chicken wings until soup just covers all ingredients. Season with sugar, cook about 5 minutes more, then put in *sake* and soy sauce and continue to boil on low heat until chicken is well-done, or about 20 minutes.

Serving
Usually boiled beans are served at room temperature, but when chicken is cooked along with beans, gelatin sometimes forms when the soup cools. Therefore, it is preferable to heat beans until the gelatin dissolves before serving.

Advice for Weight-watchers
Soybeans and soybean products are good for health because they are high in protein and low in calories, and the nonsaturated fatty acids in their oils work to reduce the amount of cholesterol in the body.
In the Japanese diet, processed soybean products such as *tofu* or *abura-age* (thin deep-fried *tofu*), rather than the beans themselves, appear on the dining table daily. Since remote times in Japan, vegetarians and Buddhist monks, who do not eat fish and meat, have maintained their health and weight because they eat a lot of products made from soybeans.
Intake of protein is a problem when trying to slim down in an attractive and healthy way. It is important to achieve a good balance between animal and vegetable protein.

Eggplant and Green Peppers Sautéed with Miso

CALORIES 197
PROTEIN .6.6g
FATS. 15.1g
CARBOHYDRATES 6.6g

Sweet Potatoes Boiled with Lemon Flavoring

CALORIES 188
PROTEIN 1.5g
FATS. 0.3g
CARBOHYDRATES 44.8g

Eggplant and Green Peppers Sautéed with Miso

Eggplant, *miso,* ginger and oil go very well together. This savory dish is a good one to serve on hot summer days when appetites are lagging. Adding a clove of garlic will make it even more zesty.

Cooking time: 15 minutes

Ingredients
5 small eggplants, about 3 ounces (80g) each
3 green peppers
½ inch (1cm) cube fresh ginger
3 tablespoons vegetable oil
4 ounces (100g) ground pork or chicken
2 teaspoons cornstarch or potato starch, plus 1½ tablespoons cold water to dissolve it

To season ingredients: ½ cup water, 1 teaspoon sugar, ⅓ teaspoon salt, 1 tablespoon soy sauce, 1 tablespoon *sake* or dry white wine, 1 tablespoon *miso*

Preparation
1. Cut eggplants into 2 x 1 inch (5 x 2.5cm) bars, making 2 to 3 shallow slashes on peel so seasoning will seep in. Soak in water immediately about 5 minutes after cutting to prevent discoloring. Drain and pat dry.
2. Quarter green peppers. Remove seeds and ribs. If pieces are large, cut again in half so they will be approximately the same size as eggplant bars.
3. Peel ginger and mince.
4. Mix all ingredients for seasoning until sugar and salt dissolve.

Cooking and Serving
1. Heat frying pan for 1 minute over high heat, then put in 3 tablespoons vegetable oil. Sauté ginger and ground meat for about 2 minutes, or until meat changes color, separating it with spatula to prevent lumping.
2. Add eggplant and sauté until almost done or for 3 to 4 minutes. Put in green pepper and sauté about 2 minutes more.
3. Next, pour seasoning all over sautéed ingredients and mix well. Dissolve cornstarch or potato starch in 1½ tablespoons cold water and stir quickly through soup to thicken it. When soup simmers again, turn off heat.
4. Serve hot on large platter or small plates.

Sweet Potatoes Boiled with Lemon Flavoring

This is a beautiful and refreshing dish which combines the sweet taste of boiled sweet potatoes with the tart flavor and fragrance of lemon. It can be used as a side dish, dessert, or snack.

Preparation, Cooking and Serving
1. Peel sweet potatoes, removing any dark spots on the skin. Cut crosswise into 1 inch (2.5cm) thick rounds. Soak in water for 10 minutes to prevent discoloring, changing the water twice. Drain.
2. Slice lemon thin.
3. Boil potatoes in water and seasonings. When half done, add lemon slices. Continue to boil until well done, or about 20 to 25 minutes, turning over occasionally.
4. Serve hot or at room temperature together with the cooked lemon slices.

Serving
Serve hot or at room temperature together with the cooked lemon slices.

Cooking time: 40 minutes

Ingredients
2 medium sweet potatoes, about 1 pound (500g)
½ lemon
1½ cups water or enough to just cover potatoes
4 tablespoons sugar
Pinch of salt

TOFU
AND OTHER DISHES

Tofu **Dishes:** *Tofu,* a product processed from soybeans, is rich in vegetable protein and calcium. The virtues of vegetable protein have been highlighted in recent years, and *tofu,* an especially excellent source of this protein, has attracted attention around the world because of its outstanding nutritional content and low calorie count.

Tofu can be eaten plain, but also goes well with many kinds of meat, fish and vegetables. Therefore, it is used for main dishes, in one-pot table cooking (see page 29), in soups and in sundry other ways.

Egg dishes: In Japanese cooking, there are many splendid dishes made with eggs. Among these, steamed dishes, including *chawan-mushi* (steamed custard containing chicken, shrimp, and vegetables) introduced in this section, are one typical variety. Steaming custard dishes over indirect heat brings to life the natural flavor of the ingredients and helps preserve their nutritional content. Moreover, since oil is not used when steaming, this cooking method results in a low-calorie dish.

Noodle dishes: The most typical of Japanese noodle dishes are *udon* and *soba.* The main ingredient of *udon* is wheat flour and of *soba,* buckwheat flour.

There are two major ways of eating Japanese-style noodles. The first is to cool them after boiling, then to dip them a little at a time into a soy sauce-based broth before eating. The second way is to put the entire portion of boiled noodles into a hot soy sauce-based broth and eat them from the broth. In this case, the noodles are usually topped with cooked meat, fish, egg, or vegetables.

Fresh Tofu with Condiments

CALORIES 92
PROTEIN 7.9g
FATS 5.0g
CARBOHYDRATES 3.6g

Sautéed Tofu Topped with Shrimp and Vegetables

CALORIES 254
PROTEIN 15.8g
FATS 14.4g
CARBOHYDRATES 15.6g

Tofu Sautéed with Ground Chicken and Vegetables

CALORIES 203
PROTEIN 13.6g
FATS. 13.7g
CARBOHYDRATES 7.4g

Sauté ginger and ground chicken in hot oil, breaking up lumps with spatula.

Add carrot and mushrooms. When done, put in *tofu*, and mix gently until heated through, being careful not to mush it.

After adding seasonings, stir in egg. Finally, put in green onions and mix well.

Fresh Tofu with Condiments

This is the most simple and popular of *tofu* dishes. You will find the refreshing taste of the *tofu* enhanced, rather than covered, by the addition of certain condiments. This cool *tofu* will satisfy you on a hot summer day better than anything else.

Preparation time: 10 minutes

Ingredients
2 blocks *tofu*
2 teaspoons soy sauce

Condiments
Fresh grated ginger
Thinly sliced long scallions
Bonito fish flakes (*katsuobushi*)
Finely stripped green *shiso* leaves

Preparation
1. Prepare small quantities of a few of the condiments, according to your taste.
2. Refrigerate *tofu* until cold.

Serving
Just before serving, cut *tofu* into 4 to 6 portions and put in individual glass bowls. Sprinkle with condiments. Dip *tofu* into side dish containing soy sauce, flavoring only slightly, and eat together with condiments.

Sautéed Tofu Topped with Shrimp and Vegetables

Top slices of *tofu* with shrimp, potato, carrot, green pepper or other items of your choice, lightly brown, then season them with a vinegar-soy sauce dressing, and you have a tofu "pizza," rich in nutrition and popular with the young.

Cooking time: 30 minutes

Ingredients
2 blocks *tofu*
1 white potato
2 ounces (50g) carrot
4 ounces (100g) small shrimp
2 *shiitake* or other fresh
   mushrooms
1 green pepper
1 egg white
4 tablespoons cornstarch or
   potato starch
2 tablespoons vegetable oil

To season shrimp: ¼ teaspoon
   salt, 1 teaspoon soy sauce,
   1 tablespoon *sake* or dry
   white wine
Vinegar-soy dressing: 2
   tablespoons soy sauce, 1
   teaspoon wine vinegar or
   slightly diluted cider vinegar

Preparation and Cooking
1. Slice each block of *tofu* horizontally into 3 layers, and wrap each with dry dish towel for 10 to 15 minutes to remove excess water.
2. Peel potato and carrot and slice very thinly. Next, cut each slice into 1 inch (2.5cm) long, needle-fine strips. Soak potato strips only in cold water immediately.
3. Peel shrimp and remove veins.
4. Remove stems from mushrooms and cut tops into fine strips.
5. Quarter green pepper lengthwise and remove seeds and ribs. Next, slice each quarter crosswise into 1 inch (2.5cm) long fine strips.
6. Mix all vegetables and shrimp with their seasoning, then add egg white and cornstarch.
7. Dust one side of each piece of *tofu* with cornstarch by shaking starch on them through a fine sieve or strainer. Then spread vegetable and shrimp mixture evenly on the slices to a thickness of ½ inch (1cm).
8. Heat large skillet with 1 tablespoon oil over high heat. Put in pieces of *tofu* top side down. Sauté 3 to 4 minutes, or until slightly browned, then turn over carefully so as not to ruin their shapes. Add 1 tablespoon oil and shake the pan for even greasing, then sauté other side 2 to 3 minutes.

Serving
Serve hot. At the table, diners pour the vinegar-soy sauce dressing over their own servings. If desired, cut each piece into 2 to 3 portions.

Cooking time: 30 minutes

Ingredients
4 dried Chinese black mushrooms
1 block *tofu*
4 ounces (100g) carrot
2 long scallions
½ inch (1cm) cube fresh ginger
1 egg
1 tablespoon vegetable oil

To season: 1 tablespoon sugar,
  2½ tablespoons soy sauce,
  2 tablespoons *sake* or dry
  white wine

Tofu Sautéed with Ground Chicken and Vegetables

This is an example of home-style *tofu* cooking with excellent nutritional balance. Because the *tofu* is broken up and cooked with meat, egg, vegetables and seasoning, even people who do not care for plain *tofu* will surely enjoy this dish.

Preparation
1. Cover mushrooms with warm water and soak 10 to 15 minutes, or until soft. Remove stems and cut tops into fine strips.
2. Break *tofu* coarsely with chopsticks or fork. Drain in sieve.
3. Julienne carrot into 1½ inch (4cm) lengths.
4. Cut green onions crosswise into ½ inch (1cm) lengths.
5. Mince ginger.
6. Stir egg well, but do not beat.
7. Mix seasonings for sautéed ingredients until sugar dissolves.

Cooking and Serving
1. Heat oil in pan over high heat and sauté ginger and ground chicken 2 to 3 minutes until meat changes color, breaking up lumps with spatula. Add carrot and mushrooms, then sauté 3 to 4 minutes more, or until carrot strips are done.
2. Add *tofu* and mix gently from the bottom until *tofu* is heated through, being careful not to mush it.
3. Pour seasonings evenly over ingredients. Put in green onion and mix well. Finally, stir in egg and turn off heat.
4. Serve hot or at room temperature in small bowls or one large bowl.

Cooking time: 30 minutes

Ingredients
4 ounces (100g) carrot
½ block or 4 ounces (100g) devil's
  tongue jelly (**konnyaku**)
4 *shiitake* or other fresh
  mushrooms
1 ounce (25g) snow peas
⅓ cup *dashi* (page 26)
1 teaspoon sugar
2 teaspoons soy sauce

Tofu dressing: 1 block tofu,
  2 tablespoons toasted sesame
  seeds, 1 tablespoon sugar,
  1 tablespoon *sake* or dry white
  wine, 1 teaspoon soy sauce,
  ⅔ teaspoon salt

Variation

Boiled Vegetables with Tofu Dressing

This *tofu* dressing is a slightly sweet one made by mashing *tofu* and adding toasted ground sesame seeds and seasoning. The combination of colorful vegetables and white dressing makes this a beautiful salad.

Preparation
1. Cut carrot into thin 1 x ¼ inch (2.5 x 0.5cm) oblong strips.
2. Cut *konnyaku* in half lengthwise, then slice each half into the same sized pieces as the carrot.
3. Remove stems from mushrooms and cut tops into fine strips.
4. Remove strings from snow peas.
Cooking and Serving
1. Boil carrot and *konnyaku* in *dashi* and seasonings for 2 to 3 minutes. Add mushrooms, boil 1 minute and drain.
2. Boil snow peas in boiling water for 2 to 3 minutes, drain and cut diagonally into fine strips.
3. Simmer block of *tofu* whole in plain boiling water for 2 minutes, and drain in cheesecloth-lined colander. After cooling slightly, squeeze water from it by twisting both edges of the cloth until most of excess water has come out. Mash, add to toasted ground sesame seeds and mix with remaining ingredients for dressing.
4. Combine all ingredients with *tofu* dressing just before serving. Mound in small bowls.

Steamed Custard with Chicken, Shrimp and Vegetables

CALORIES 213
PROTEIN 21.7g
FATS. 11.9g
CARBOHYDRATES 3.4g

Noodles Cooked with Chicken and Vegetables

CALORIES 611
PROTEIN 25.9g
FATS. 16.3g
CARBOHYDRATES 17.6g

Cooking time: 40 minutes

Steamed Custard with Chicken, Shrimp and Vegetables

You will find this custard ideal for guests because of its lovely colors. Make it into a "new dish" each time just by changing the serving containers. Instead of fish stock, try chicken soup occasionally or experiment with new ingredients.

Ingredients

6 ounces (150g) chicken, bones and skin removed
1 teaspoon soy sauce
1 teaspoon *sake* or dry white wine
8 medium shrimp
4 *shiitake* or other fresh mushrooms
2 ounces (50g) carrot
4 leaves fresh spinach
1 inch (2.5cm) square piece lemon rind
4 eggs

Broth: 2½ cups *dashi* (page 26), 1 teaspoon salt, 1½ teaspoons soy sauce, 1 tablespoon *sake* or dry white wine

Utensils

Steamer or large, deep pot with tight-fitting lid
Small cuplike bowls or coffee cups

Preparation

1. Heat broth until salt dissolves and cool thoroughly.
2. Cut chicken into 1 inch (2.5cm) squares. Preflavor with soy sauce and *sake* or dry white wine and let stand 10 minutes.
3. Peel shrimp, but leave each tail and just the last section of shell nearest each tail attached to help maintain the shape of the shrimp while cooking. Remove veins by inserting a toothpick under vein at center of the back and pulling up gently.
4. Remove stems from mushrooms. If tops are large, cut in half or quarter.
5. Slice carrot into thin rounds. If big, cut pieces in half.
6. Bring to boil a small amount of water containing a pinch of salt. Put in spinach and boil, without lid, about 2 minutes. Drain, then cut into 1 inch (2.5cm) lengths.
7. Cut lemon rind into fine strips.
8. Mix eggs well with chopsticks, fork, or gently with small whisk, but do not beat. Stir broth into eggs little by little, and mix gently so as not to generate bubbles. Strain through fine sieve or cheesecloth-lined strainer to remove slippery substance from egg white.
9. Divide all ingredients, except egg-broth mixture and lemon rind, into 4 portions and put each attractively into cups. Ladle ¼ of egg-broth mixture into each, leaving at least a ½ inch (1cm) space between it and the top of the cup.

Cooking and Serving

1. If using steamer put water in pan under steamer. If using an ordinary pot, put in about 2½ cups water. Bring to boil, then turn off heat for a moment. Place cups containing ingredients inside steamer or pot, leaving a little space between each cup to let steam circulate well, then heat up again over medium heat with a dry dish towel under lid to absorb steam.
2. When water simmers again, reduce heat to very low and loosen lid slightly so the temperature inside the pot does not rise too high. Too much heat will make the custard spongy. Continue to steam for 15 to 20 minutes.
3. Stick a fine skewer into center of custard. If skewer comes up clean, the custard is done. Put in lemon rind for decoration and turn off heat.
4. Serve hot with saucers under cups.

Advice for Weight-watchers

No oil is required to cook the eggs in this low-calorie dish. Regulate the number of calories by adjusting the ingredients and make this into the ideal diet food. Changing items or reducing their volume will not effect the flavor of the tasty fish stock base.

Cooking time: 40 minutes

Ingredients
**14 ounces (400g) thick, dried
  Japanese wheat noodles (*udon*)
7 ounces (200g) chicken, boned
  and skin left on or removed
1 teaspoon soy sauce
1 teaspoon *sake* or dry white wine
2 ounces (50g) carrot
4 to 8 *shiitake* or other fresh
  mushrooms
4 ounces (100g) fresh spinach
2 long scallions or 1 leek
4 eggs
Seven-flavored cayenne (*shichimi
  togarashi*)**

**To precook ingredients: ⅔ cup
  dashi (page 26) or water, ½
  teaspoon sugar, 1 teaspoon soy
  sauce
Final broth: 5 cups *dashi* (page
  26), 5 tablespoons soy sauce, 3
  tablespoons *mirin*, ½ teaspoon
  salt**

Utensils
**Individual earthenware pots or
  flameproof casserole dishes
  (shallow)**

Noodles Cooked with Chicken and Vegetables

This dish is perfect for cold winter weather. Cook it in individual serving containers, carry them to the table and eat directly from them. If you do not have small individual containers, cook it in one large container, then divide it at the table.

Preparation
1. Bring 8 cups water to boil, put in noodles little by little, separating them from each other with chopsticks or fork to prevent them from sticking together. When water bubbles up again, add ½ cup cold water to check the bubbling action and to prevent the surface of the noodles from becoming too soft and frayed. When water simmers again, repeat this procedure 2 more times, and cook until noodles are almost done, or for 10 to 12 minutes. Cooking time will depend on the thickness of noodles, so follow instructions on the package. Do not overcook, because they will be slightly heated again just before serving. Pour into colander, rinse under running water and cover with damp dishcloth until use.
2. Cut chicken into 1 inch (2.5cm) squares. Preflavor with soy sauce and *sake* and let stand 10 minutes.
3. Cut carrot crosswise into thin rounds.
4. Remove stems from mushrooms. Carve crisscross design on tops.
5. Bring pan of water to boil, add a pinch of salt and cook spinach about 2 minutes and drain. Cool under running water, gently squeeze out excess water, and cut into 1 inch (2.5cm) lengths.
6. Cut green onions crosswise into 1 inch (2.5cm) lengths.

Cooking and Serving
1. Boil carrot in ⅔ cup *dashi,* or water, with ½ teaspoon sugar and 1 teaspoon soy sauce until half-done, or about 2 minutes, then add chicken and boil 2 minutes more. Last, add mushrooms and boil 1 minute.
2. Mix ingredients for final broth and bring to boil. When ready, put 1 ladle of broth into each individual earthenware serving pot, then into each pot ¼ of noodles. Divide carrot, chicken, spinach, green onion and mushrooms evenly among pots, arranging them attractively on top of noodles. Last, pour ¼ of remaining broth over each.
3. Heat pots over low-to-medium heat. When they begin to boil, break an egg into the center, put the lid on, and turn off heat. In a minute the egg will be half-done. If you prefer a well-done egg, heat a little longer.
4. Transfer pots to table, placing them on heat protectors or mats. Sprinkle contents with condiment and eat directly from pots.

Advice for Weight-watchers
This is a diet noodle dish. You can cut down on the number of calories without appreciably affecting nutritional content simply by reducing the quantity of noodles and leaving the amount of the other ingredients unchanged. Drinking a good portion of the soup will also leave you with a feeling of fullness and satisfaction.

Japanese Vegetables

Chinese cabbage (*hakusai*)

Long scallion (*negi*)

Scallions (*wakegi*)

Chives (*asatsuki*)

Japanese-type cucumber (*kyuri*)

Eggplant (*nasu*)

Trefoil (*mitsuba*)

Lotus root (*renkon*)

Canned *renkon*

Canned *gobo*

Burdock root (*gobo*)

Long white radish (*daikon*)

Japanese-type pumpkin (*kabocha*)

Bamboo shoots (*takenoko*)

Canned *takeno*

Ginger shoots (*ha-shoga*)

Fresh ginger (*shoga*)

Snow peas (*saya-endo*)

Bottled *ha-shoga*

Mushrooms (*shiitake*): from the left, dried in package, the same and raw

Beefsteak plant (*shiso*)

Photos by Hajime Masuo

98

Japanese Vegetables

Daikon (long white radish): This white root grows rather large in length and girth and has a lot of meat and juice. Its leaves have an unusually large amount of vitamin C, so by all means should be used. *Daikon* are marketed year round and are grouped by their season of harvest. Especially delicious are the fall and winter ones. They are used primarily in boiled dishes and for pickling, grating, marinating in vinegary sauce (see page 79), or as condiment for *sashimi*. Spring and summer *daikon* differ from fall and winter ones only in that they are hotter in taste but weaker in flavor.

Gobo (burdock root): Its fragrance is good, and it is pleasantly chewable. The skin portion is especially fragrant and delicious. This root can be cleaned by rubbing the skin with a brush and washing, but the thinnest possible layer of skin can be removed by just scraping lightly with the back of a knife. After scraping, the root will soon begin to change color, so should be cut right away according to its intended use and immediately soaked in a large amount of water to avoid discoloration. It is used in dishes boiled with flavorings *(nimono)*, is deep fried or added to soups or pickled dishes.

Hakusai (Chinese cabbage): Recently this vegetable can be seen the year-around, but its season is winter. It is characterized by a high water content, soft fibers, and a flavor with no strong peculiarities. The leaves form a compact bundle and come off layer by layer from the base. Those heads with no specks on the leaves are of good quality. Together with long white radish *(daikon)*, it is pickled in winter, but is also used a lot in one-pot table cooking *(nabemono)*.

Kabocha (Japanese-type pumpkin): There are many varieties, but most have a flat, globular shape. They can be substituted with a winter squash such as acorn. Their meat is fleshy and highly palatable. They also grow easily and store well. Those high in quality are heavy proportionate to their size, the meat is compact, and the skin is hard and looks as if it had been scratched with claws. Primarily, it is boiled with seasonings or sliced and deep fried. One should be careful that the seeds and inside pulp are properly cleaned or the meat will develop a bad smell.

Kyuri (Japanese-type cucumber): There are approximately 50 varieties distinguished by the color of skin, shape, mode of cultivation, and so forth, but little difference in flavor by type. The Japanese cucumber compared to the American variety typically used in salads is smaller around and roughly ⅓ its overall size. The skin is softer but the pulp less juicy and more firm all the way through, and it contains hardly any seeds. Those with vivid green color, straight shape, firm body and taut skin are the best choices. They are used in vinegared dishes *(sunomono),* for pickling *(tsukemono),* or in salads.

Mitsuba (trefoil): This is a time-honored vegetable in Japan. Its height is about 12 to 20 inches (30–50cm), and its delicate stalk branches have 3 leaves, hence its name "tre-foil." It has a unique fragrance, and the color of its leaves is particularly beautiful. It is delicious boiled very lightly, then dressed, or added as coloring to soups or small Japanese-style side dishes.

Nasu (eggplant): Its history of cultivation is long, so there are many varieties, but they can be divided by shape into round type and long type. There are no differences in product quality based on shape. They are best when the calyx is fresh, there are no bruises, the color of the skin is dark purple and has a nice gloss. They are delicious deep fried or sautéed and also tasty pickled. A Japanese eggplant is very roughly ¼ to ⅕ the size of its American counterpart.

Negi (long scallion): There are two main types. One *(ha-negi),* most of which is green, has cylindrical leaves and stem and is eaten primarily for its green part. The other *(nebuka-negi),* the major part of which is white, has hard leaves and is eaten primarily for the white stem part. It is slightly smaller in diameter but more pithy than a leek. Both types are used in the same way—as an ingredient for *sukiyaki* and other one-pot table cooking *(nabemono)* and as a condiment for soups and noodle dishes. The characteristic fragrance of onion is also useful for killing the smell of fish and meat.

Asatsuki (chives): This variety of *negi* resembles chives in appearance. Eaten when it reaches a length of 4 to 6 inches (10–15cm), it is a delicate onion with mild flavor and fragrance. It is cut finely and used as condiment and to add coloring to soups.

Wakegi (scallions): Its length is from 8 to 12 inches (20–30cm). It is thinner and softer and its fragrance weaker than that of *negi*. It is used in about the same way as *negi*, but is especially delicious boiled for a second or two and added to Japanese-style side dishes.

Renkon (lotus root): This is the root stock of the aquatic lotus plant. They are rich in starch and vitamin C. The roots are of good quality when the skin surface is cream-colored, the shape is nice, the holes are small in size and number, and the meat thick. They have a faint bitter taste so should be soaked in water with a little vinegar to remove the harshness. They are used widely in dishes boiled with flavorings *(nimono)*, vinegared dishes *(sunomono),* and small Japanese-style side dishes.

Saya-endo (snow peas): Snow peas are one variety of shell pea with edible shell. The shells are small, smooth and glossy, juicy and soft. After the strings have been removed and they are cooked in salted boiling water, snow peas are dressed (called *ohitashi*), added to Japanese-style side dishes *(aemono),* or used as garnish for dishes boiled with flavorings *(nimono)*.

Shiitake (fresh or dried black mushrooms): The diameter of the cap is 1½ to 4 inches (4–10cm), and the surface black-brown in color. They are rich in vitamins B_2 and D. These mushrooms are sold raw or dried; the dried ones are better in flavor and aroma. The dried ones are of good quality if the stems are short and small in diameter, the mushroom is well-dried, and the cap emits a lot of liquor when soaked. The raw ones are used for steamed dishes, in one-pot table cooking *(nabemono)*, soups, and so forth, and the dried ones for rice dishes and Japanese-style vegetable side dishes.

Shiso leaves (beefsteak plant; perilla): There are two types—one with purple-red leaves *(aka-jiso)* and another with green leaves *(ao-jiso)*. When the surface of the leaf is puckered like crepe, the quality is good and the fragrance will be nice. The green variety is the one most commonly used in cooking. The leaf is cut finely and mixed with rice or with vegetables being pickled, or is served whole as a complement to *sashimi*.

Shoga (fresh ginger): The edible part of the plant is the root. Because it has a characteristic strong flavor and delightful aroma, it is widely used both as a seasoning and condiment. Pickled ginger shoots *(ha-shoga)* are served as a complement to grilled fish and other dishes, while fully grown ginger root *(ne-shoga)* is cut into needle-fine strips or grated and used to kill the smell of fish or meat in dishes boiled with flavorings *(nimono)*. It is always served together with *sushi* and certain *tofu* dishes as condiment.

Takenoko (bamboo shoots): "Bamboo shoots" is the general name given to the buds which stick out from the lower branches of the bamboo tree, but more specifically it refers to the shoots from the lower part of the specie of bamboo called *mosochiku (Phyllostachys pubescens)*. The shoot is thick, and on the surface of the skin can be seen what looks like fine velvety hairs. The shoots are boiled, then the leaf-like layers are peeled off and the inside meat eaten. Because the meat is soft and the flavor mild, it can be used in many kinds of dishes, but is especially delicious in dishes boiled with flavorings *(nimono)* and in Japanese-style vegetable side dishes.

Grains, Seaweed Varieties and Processed Foods

Rice *(kome)*

Buckwheat noodles *(soba)*

Dried *udon* (eaten cold)

Thick, Japanese-style wheat noodles *(udon)*: top and center, dried (usually eaten hot), below, raw

Dried laver (varieties of *nori*)

A powdered form *(ao-nori)*

From the left, dried kelp *(konbu)* and extract of kelp *(konbu-dashi)*

Bean threads *(harusame)*

Dried bonito *(katsuo-bushi)*

A kind of seaweed *(wakame)*

Dried gourd strips *(kampyo)*

From the left, varieties of shaved bonito *(kezuri-bushi)* and extract of bonito *(katsuo-dashi)*

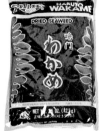

Thin, deep-fried *tofu* *(abura-age)*

Thick, deep-fried *tofu* *(atsu-age)*

Bean curd *(tofu)*

Below, translucent, jelly-like block (varieties of *konnyaku*); above left, shredded thick noodles, right, *shirataki*

Grains, Seaweed Varieties, and Processed Foods

Harusame (bean threads): *Harusame* is made from various starches, most commonly Chinese *mung* beans, and comes in the form of fine, translucent filaments. High-quality products do not break apart when boiled. Before using, they are softened in boiling hot water and commonly added to vinegared dishes (*sunomono*), one-pot dishes cooked at the table (*nabemono*), and so forth.

Kampyo (dried gourd strips): The flesh of the 24 to 36 inch (60–90cm) gourd (*yugao*) is peeled off into long thin strips and dried. Good-quality strips are white in color, of uniform thickness, well-dried, and have a characteristic sweet aroma. To prepare, they are first rinsed in water, rubbed with salt, then soaked in lukewarm water for 15 minutes. They are then cooked in boiling water until soft, then flavor is added. Besides being used often in *sushi* dishes (e.g., *gomoku-zushi, nori-maki*), the strips are also utilized in boiled dishes to which flavoring is added (*nimono*).

Katsuobushi (shaved dried bonito fish flakes): The head, tail, and bones are removed from the bonito, and the meat is cut into three pieces using filleting techniques. They are steam-processed, then dried into extremely hard blocks. These are shaved thin with a "bonito shaver," and the flakes are used to make soup stock for soups and boiled dishes and also to add flavor to side dishes. Good-quality blocks are those which feel hard and heavy, have a luster on the surface, their red meat sections are a black-brown color, and two of them tapped together make a clear hard sound. When shaved in advance, it is called *kezuri-bushi*. If left in the open air, oxygen will cause product quality to deteriorate rapidly. Therefore, the commercial products are sold in vacuum-packed containers.

Kome (uncooked rice): In the Japanese diet, rice is a staple seldom omitted at mealtime. The part of a grain of rice that is left after the chaff has been removed is called *genmai*, or unpolished rice. Ordinary white rice is *genmai* from which the seed coat (bran layer) has been removed or, in other words, polished rice. Throughout the areas of the world, a large number of varieties of rice are cultivated. Distinguished by shape of kernel, the Japanese form is short and roundish, while slim long rice is the most common form outside Asia. Distinguished by method of cultivation, there is the wetland rice plant grown in irrigated paddies and the upland rice plant grown in dry fields. In addition, rice can be divided into glutinous and nonglutinous types according to the difference in nature of the kernel's starch, which is the principal ingredient of rice. In Japan, nonglutinous wet-land rice is used almost exclusively. There are many people who think that rice is good as a "beauty food," but eaten by itself, it is nutritionally insufficient. Certainly the nutritional value of rice is high but, notwithstanding, it should be combined with a main dish or side dish to achieve a well-balanced diet.

Konbu (dried kelp): *Konbu* is a variety of seaweed. It is used in the making of fish soup stock and in boiled, flavored dishes. It is of good quality when it has a gloss, is black or greenish-brown in color, has a white powdery-looking substance on its surface, and is thick. When prepared, *konbu* should not be rinsed but should only be wiped with a cloth to remove sand. Besides fish stock, it is used in boiled dishes, marinated and wrapped in bundles and tied with gourd strips (*konbu-maki*), or boiled down in soy sauce and seasonings and used as highly seasoned side dishes (*tsukudani*).

Konnyaku (translucent, jelly-like block made from starch of root called "devil's tongue"): The plant from which this product is made is called *konnyaku imo*. *Konnyaku* has attracted public attention as a "beauty food" in recent years because it is a low-calorie food. It cannot be digested by the body so is passed through. Thus, it helps to cleanse the intestinal tract, but it should not be eaten in large quantities. While it is low in calories, it is also low in nutritional value. Thus, to use it as a "beauty food," it must naturally be used in combination with other foods. As milk of lime is used in the manufacturing process to solidify it, the *konnyaku* is usually boiled before eating to remove the smell of lime. It is almost always used in boiled or dressed dishes.

Shirataki (translucent, jelly-like noodles): These are thin filaments made by shredding *konnyaku*. They are used mainly as an ingredient for one-pot dishes boiled at the table (*nabemono*) or in dressed dishes (*aemono*).

Nori (dried laver): This is the processed leaf parts of a soft seaweed called laver. It is a low-calorie food containing a lot of iodine and carotin (a source of vitamin A). It is toasted over heat until it gives off a fragrant aroma and becomes slightly crisp. In *sushi*, in particular, it is an essential ingredient. It is also used in deep-fried dishes to add aroma and flavor, or on rice and noodle dishes as condiment. An already toasted *nori* (called *yaki-nori*) is presently sold on the market. Other ready-to-use *nori* products are *aji-tsuke-nori*, a seasoned, dried laver; *ao-nori*, a powdered form used to sprinkle on food; *nori* boiled down in soy sauce with seasonings (*nori-tsukudani*); and so forth.

Soba (buckwheat noodles): Soba noodles are sometimes made from pure buckwheat flour, but commonly starch, egg, and so forth, are added as binding agents. Water is added to the flour, it is made into a dough, kneaded and pounded out, then cut thin. In Japan *soba* is sold in 3 forms—raw (*nama-soba*), boiled (*yude-soba*), and dried (*hoshi-soba*). After boiling, a soy sauce-based broth (*soba-tsuyu*) is poured over the noodles or they are dipped little by little into the broth which is served in a side dish. Customarily, finely sliced onion or the hot red pepper-based spice *shichimi togarashi* are served with them as condiments.

Tofu (bean curd): This food product is processed from soybeans. Containing high-quality protein, oil and calcium, its nutritional value is high. The soybeans are soaked well in water and mashed. The milky soybean whey is drawn off the mash and heated, then a solidifying agent is added. It is caused to coagulate, then is poured into a mold and the water drained off. Typical *tofu* dishes are cold *tofu* (*hiya-yakko*) and boiled *tofu* (*yu-dofu*), both served with condiments. It is also widely used in soups, one-pot table cooking (*nabemono*), dressed dishes (*aemono*), and in countless other ways.

Abura-age (thin, deep-fried tofu): *Tofu* is sliced thin, cut to a fixed size, its water removed, then it is deep fried in oil. There is a thin type (*usu-age*) and a thick type (*atsu-age*). When people say *abura-age*, they are referring to the thin type. When of good quality, it has elasticity, a sheen on both sides and is moist. Before using, hot water is poured over it, and the excess oil on the surface is wiped off. It is used as an ingredient in various types of cooking, such as boiled dishes, *miso* soup, and rice and noodle dishes.

Udon (thick, Japanese-style wheat noodles): These noodles are made by combining flour and a small quantity of salt, adding water, then forming a dough and kneading well. The dough is pounded out, then chopped into moderately thick noodles. After boiling, the noodles are usually eaten with a soy sauce-based broth poured over them or dipped into a broth which is served in a side dish. They are usually accompanied by condiments such as finely sliced onion or a hot red pepper-based spice mixture called *shichimi togarashi* (literally, 7-flavored cayenne). Variations of *udon* are *hiyamugi*, usually eaten cold, and *somen*, a very fine delicate noodle. They are distinguished not only by their size but also by method of preparation.

Wakame (a kind of seaweed): *Wakame* is a 24- to 40-inch (60–100cm) seaweed somewhat similar to laver (*nori*). A low-calorie food product rich in iodine and calcium, it is sold raw, partially dried and salted, and fully dried. Before using, it is rinsed in water to remove the salt and then soaked in new water until soft. It is used in salads, boiled dishes, soups, vinegared dishes, (*sunomono*), and so on.

Seasonings, Spices and Seeds

Soy sauce (shoyu): from the left, regular 150ml, 250ml; light; low-salt 500ml, 250ml

(mirin): left, ordinary (hon-mirin); right, flavor-added (aji-mirin)

Rice wine (sake)

Vinegar (su): left, brewed (yone-zu); right, flavor-added (sushi-zu)

From the left, soup base for noodles and tempura (memmi), sukiyaki sauce, teriyaki sauce, extract of bonito (katsuo-dashi), extract of kelp (konbu-dashi)

Varieties of soybean paste (miso)

Japanese horseradish (fresh wasabi)

wasabi powder

From the left, white sesame seeds, black sesame seeds and sesame seed oil (goma-abura)

Left, prickly ash seed with coat (mi-zansho); right, spice made of seed coat (sansho)

Dried red peppers (togarashi)

7-flavored cayenne pepper (shichimi-togarashi)

102

Seasonings, Spices and Seeds

Goma (sesame seeds): These are the flattish seeds of the sesame herb. There are 3 types distinguished by color— black, white, and brown. With the black variety, the seeds are large and the yield high, but their quality and oil content are comparatively low. With the white variety, the seeds are small and yield low, but quality is high. They, therefore, measure up better as food than do the black ones. Brown sesame seeds are similar to the black ones. The type of seed used and the way it is used vary according to the type of dish. The seeds are used whole or lightly toasted and ground. When used freshly ground in dressed dishes and sesame dipping sauces, their distinctive flavor and aroma can be fully appreciated. .

Goma-abura (sesame seed oil): Made from sesame seeds, which are rich in oil and protein, this oil has a unique taste and aroma. It is mixed with salad oil and used for frying *tempura* or used to add flavor and aroma to Japanese-style dressed dishes *(aemono)*.

Mirin (sweet rice wine for cooking): This is a type of alcohol made from sweet glutinous short-grained rice *(mochigome)* and known as *hon-mirin*. Its alcohol content ranges between 13 and 22 percent, and its sugar content between 25 and 38 percent. The combination of alcohol and sugar gives *mirin* a distinctive flavor and sweetness. *Mirin* is never used for drinking; it is used primarily to add sweet flavor to cooking, such as to boiled or grilled dishes, or to add taste and sheen. In addition to *hon-mirin* above, there are also processed varieties which contain seasonings. These flavor-added varieties are called *aji-mirin*.

Miso (soybean paste): A characteristic seasoning in Japanese cooking, this semi-solid paste is made by fermenting soybeans. Differentiated according to the type of malt added to the soybean mash, there are rice *miso (kome-miso)*, barley *miso (mugi-miso)* and soybean *miso (mame-miso)*. Distinguished also by the content of salt and starch used, as well as color tone, there are many varieties. Besides being used for *miso* soup, it finds use in dressed dishes *(aemono)*, grilled and fried foods, one-pot table cookery, preserved dishes *(misozuke)*, and so forth. Since contact with air will cause a gradual change of flavor, *miso* should be kept in an air-tight container and put in a cool dark place.

Sake (rice wine): Usually called *Nihonshu* (Japanese wine) or *sake*, it is brewed using rice as the major ingredient and has an alcoholic content of 15 to 17 percent. *Sake* is divided into 3 grades—special *(tokkyu)*, first *(ikkyu)* and second *(nikyu)*. It is used mainly as an alcoholic drink, but for seasoning food, second grade is commonly employed. Used somewhat like sweet cooking *sake (mirin)*, it acts as a hidden flavor in boiled and sautéed dishes, in one-pot table cookery *(nabemono)*, baked dishes, and so on, and is used to add a finishing touch to cooking.

Sansho powder (spice of the prickly ash): The outside covering of the completely ripe *sansho* seed is dried and this covering is made into powder. It has a unique aroma and prickly hot yet mild spiciness different from any one spice in Western cooking. It is used as a spice in soups, on broiled eel, and so forth. Unripe *sansho* seeds with jacket on *(mizansho)* are used as an ingredient in preserved foods boiled down with soy sauce *(tsukudani)*.

Shichimi togarashi (7-flavored cayenne): To very hot powdered red pepper, *sansho*, flax, poppy and black sesame seeds, *chenpi* (dried tangerine peel), and *shiso* (beefsteak plant) seeds are added in appropriate quantity to create this hot spice. It is used sparingly to season noodle dishes, in one-pot table cookery *(nabemono)*, for *yakitori*, and so on.

Aka-togarashi (red pepper): There are many varieties, but they can be broken down into two major groups—sweet and hot. The hot type, the one most generally used as seasoning is called *aka-togarashi*. The pod of "red" peppers are green when young but turn red when they mature. The dried pods are used in cooking, but since the seeds are very hot, they are taken out and the pod is cut up. These are added as hot flavoring to pickled and boiled vegetables and are also used sometimes when boiling fish to kill the fishy smell.

Shoyu (soy sauce): This is the most prominent liquid seasoning used in Japanese cooking. There are many varieties, but the most commonly used are *koi-kuchi-shoyu* (regular soy sauce) and *usu-kuchi-shoyu* (light-colored soy sauce). By far the most popular brand in Japan is Kikkoman.
Koi-kuchi-shoyu (regular Kikkoman Soy Sauce) is most versatile. It has a deep, reddish-brown color, a rich, complex flavor and a savory aroma. These characteristics are achieved by using equal parts of soybeans and wheat in the mash, and a fermentation period of more than 6 months under careful microbial control to encourage enzyme action and to mature the mash completely. Because soy sauce has a splendid flavor and aroma, it can be used in various kinds of cooking and with many kinds of ingredients, including fish dishes to kill the smell.
Gen-en-shoyu or low-salt soy sauce (Kikkoman Milder Soy Sauce) is brewed in the traditional way to give it the flavor of regular Kikkoman Soy Sauce. Then, about 43% of the salt is removed. Its use need not be limited to those who must reduce their sodium consumption. It is recommended for use as a recipe ingredient as well as a table condiment.
Usu-kuchi-shoyu (Kikkoman Light Color Soy Sauce) is brewed similarly to regular Kikkoman Soy Sauce but under stricter controls to reduce the intensity of the color. The result is about one-fourth the color of regular soy sauce. It is used where it is not desirable to darken the natural color of ingredients, such as light-colored vegetables and meats. It can also be used in preparing *sumashi-jiru* (clear soup) and one-pot meals such as *yosenabe*.
In addition to the above, there is also *tamari-shoyu* made only with soybeans as opposed to regular soy sauce which uses soybeans and wheat as main ingredients. It is employed for special uses, such as in *sushi* restaurants, but not for common use in the home.

Su (vinegar): This sour seasoning contains 3 to 5 percent acetic acid. There are brewed and synthetic types, but the synthetic ones are less mild and sweet than the brewed ones and are more sour. Among the brewed types, most often used in cooking, those made from rice *(yone-zu)* and *sake* lees *(kasu-zu)* are the most common. Vinegar is an essential ingredient in making *sushi*, vinegared dishes *(sunomono)* and in pickling. In addition to these, it is employed in a wide range of other uses—to suppress the smell of fish, to prevent discoloration of peeled vegetables, such as burdock root and lotus root, to soften bones in small fish when boiled, and so on.

Teriyaki sauce: Made from naturally brewed soy sauce by adding wine, vinegar, spices and sugar, this sauce is very useful for *teriyaki*, *yakitori* and all other types of barbecued and grilled dishes as a marinade, baste or seasoning.

Sukiyaki sauce: A soy sauce-based seasoning with sugar and rice wine added, this sauce is very convenient for *sukiyaki* cooking.

Memmi (A soup base for noodles and tempura): Made from naturally brewed soy sauce, with sugar, bonito extract and rice wine added, this concentrate is made into soup stock by simply diluting with hot or cold water. It is employed as a seasoning for noodle soups or as a dipping sauce for *tempura*.

Katsuo-dashi (a liquid bonito extract) and **konbu-dashi** (a liquid kelp extract): Both made from natural ingredients, these concentrates are useful for making *dashi* (soup stock), which is essential for many traditional Japanese dishes such as soups and boiled foods.

Wasabi (Japanese horseradish): This green root is hot and has a strong aroma. It is sold as a seasoning in raw, powdered, or paste form ready for use. When used raw, it is grated; thick, young fresh roots, when grated, seem a little sticky. Those freshly green in color are of good quality. The powdered form is dissolved in water and made into a paste. It is used sparingly with *sashimi* and hand-formed *sushi (nigiri-zushi)*, dressed dishes *(aemono)*, and so forth.

Japanese Cooking and Soy Sauce

Kikkoman Soy Sauce–A Long History

Brewed soy sauce originated in the Orient 2,500 years ago. The fermentation process for traditional Japanese soy sauce had achieved a high level as early as the 16th century.

Kikkoman Soy Sauce was first produced in 1630. It has gained a high reputation as an "all-purpose seasoning." Indispensable for all kinds of present-day Japanese cooking, Kikkoman Soy Sauce also goes well with many other types of dishes from around the world. Besides being used at the table, it is used as an ingredient in marinades and basting sauces, is combined with other seasonings for stews, or is added to foods like soups and casseroles.

How Does Kikkoman Soy Sauce Gain its Flavor, Color, Taste and Aroma?

The secret of Kikkoman's reputation for quality lies in its manufacturing which begins with a dry mash *(koji)* making process in which equal parts of cooked soybeans and roasted wheat are combined and a starter added. To make the wet mash and start the brewing process, an amount of salt water (brine) approximately equal to the quantity of the dry mash is added.

Through enzyme action of microorganisms in the wet mash *(moromi)*, soybean protein is changed into amino acids, giving Kikkoman its special tastiness. During this process, enzymes change the wheat starch to sugar, giving the soy sauce its sweetness, while fermentation changes some of the sugar to different acids producing a tartness. Subsequent reactions occur between sugar and amino acids to give the soy sauce its distinctive color. In addition to these changes of substance during the period of fermentation and maturation, which are brought out by the action of specific yeasts growing in the wet mash, some of the sugar changes to alcohol and its derivatives producing soy sauce's distinctive aroma. The formation of amino acids, sugar, alcohol and various acids which together create the flavor, color and aroma of Kikkoman Soy Sauce is the result of a brewing period of more than 6 months during which microbial action is carefully controlled.

Chemically made, nonbrewed soy sauce, in contrast to naturally brewed soy sauce, is produced within a few days from chemically-hydrolyzed plant protein by using hydrochloric acid at a high temperature, diluting with salt water, and then adding corn syrup, caramel coloring and other additives. Semi-chemically made soy sauce is produced by combining the above two methods.

Why is Kikkoman Called the "Liquid Spice"?

Kikkoman Soy Sauce contains more than 280 different aroma components, which accounts for its rich, complex and savory aroma. For example, one of its main aroma components is vanilla, which is also contained in whisky, brandy, coffee, chocolate, and wine. Many other aroma components of Kikkoman are found in fruits and flowers. Thus, Kikkoman Soy Sauce is often called the "liquid spice." Its subtle but complex flavor harmonizes with the natural flavors of food, never overpowering or detracting from them.

How to Preserve the Fine Quality of Kikkoman

Kikkoman Soy Sauce is naturally brewed like wine. After opening a bottle, the cap should be tightly closed and, preferably, the bottle should be refrigerated or put in a cool place. High temperature and direct exposure to air over a long time can cause the quality of soy sauce to deteriorate, especially its flavor and aroma. Heat and air can also turn the color darker by causing components to oxidize. It is, therefore, preferable to use purchased soy sauce within a month, always keeping it in a cool place so that its fine quality can be enjoyed every day.

This structure, built in the style of an old Japanese castle, is one of the Kikkoman Corporation's soy sauce-brewing facilities in Noda City, Chiba Prefecture, Japan. Called "GOYOGURA," it produces Kikkoman Soy Sauce in the traditional way exclusively for Imperial Household use.

This photo shows Kikkoman Foods, Inc., a soy sauce plant constructed in 1973 in Walworth, Wisconsin, in the United States. From this plant, Kikkoman products are supplied to the American and European markets.

How to Plan Meals for Health and Fitness

Japanese cooking is increasingly attracting the notice of people who are overweight, people with medical problems accompanying obesity, and those who desire to improve their figures or skin tone through more careful attention to their eating habits. In America and Europe, for example, *sushi* restaurants and other Japanese eating establishments are flourishing. *Tofu* and short-grained rice, and other Japanese cooking ingredients, such as *nori* (laver) and *konbu* (kelp), are becoming popular items at the checkout counter. *Sushi* and *tofu* have even become popularly known as health foods.

WHAT MAKES JAPANESE FOOD HEALTHFUL?
Rice, fish, fresh vegetables, as well as soybean products (typified by *tofu*), which are so basic to Japanese cooking, are not only nutritionally excellent foods but are also low in calories. Additionally, the methods used for cooking them are excellent for keeping the calorie count down at no sacrifice in flavor. The most conspicuous feature of Japanese cooking is that few dishes contain high-calorie fats. Inasmuch as stress is placed on bringing out the natural flavors of the ingredients, it is basic not to add anything to them beyond what is deemed necessary. Fish and shellfish of the utmost degree of freshness are eaten raw as *sashimi*. Also, many dishes are prepared using such low-calorie methods as boiling, grilling, baking, steaming, and cooking in broth with seasonings until the flavors are absorbed. Indispensable to these main methods of cooking are soy sauce, *miso* paste, *sake* (rice wine), rice vinegar and *mirin* (sweet rice wine for cooking), which are the most characteristic seasonings used in Japanese cooking and which enhance still more the natural flavors that the ingredients hold. Looked at from the nutritional standpoint, Japanese cooking offers the possibility of a moderate intake of carbohydrates while avoiding overconsumption of fats, and provides an opportunity for a balanced intake of animal and vegetable protein.

PUTTING A TOUCH OF JAPAN INTO WESTERN COOKING
In the Japanese home, the dominant pattern for generations has been the one-soup, three-dish meal. "One soup, three dishes" means a menu consisting of one bowl of soup plus one main dish and two side ones, with the soup being either *miso* or a clear soup, the main dish being fish, or meat, or some other high-protein source prepared by a cooking method that renders it low-calorie, and the side dishes consisting of foods centered around such items as vegetables and beans. In addition, rice is served as a staple.

It is the objective of this book to weave Japanese cooking into the Western diet. The Western diet, however, typically contains milk products which are not a part of the traditional Japanese meal of one soup and three dishes. Since milk products contain many good nutritional elements, their addition in the diet would be a plus. Introducing them, however, and at the same time achieving a balance of tastes within the meal poses a problem, since meals in Japan are centered on rice as the main staple. Accordingly, a menu plan has been prepared that includes bread, pasta, cereal, and other items as the main staples for breakfast and lunch, but adopts the low-calorie Japanese meal of one soup and three dishes for dinner.

In present-day Japan, eating styles have become Westernized, and in a typical day it is not uncommon for people to eat one style for one meal and another style at the next. From the viewpoint of nutrition, this varied eating pattern helps guarantee an ideal balance. By making Japanese cooking a basic part of your meal plans, you can achieve a greater balance in your eating habits.

Basic Tips for Dieting

On the previous page it was noted that Japanese cooking is good for the health and excellent as diet food. Yet the fact remains that no matter what style of food a person settles on, losing weight attractively and in a healthful way is hardly possible unless the mechanism of loss and gain is properly understood. Injury to the health can also accompany a reduction in weight over and above what is necessary. Take a close second look at your eating habits before embarking on a reducing program.

Overeating is the Cause of 95 Percent of People's Weight Problems

Being overweight is not just simply a matter of what one eats or drinks. Rather, it is a state which occurs when the amount of potential energy contained in food taken in exceeds the amount of energy expended by the body. In other words, becoming overweight results from taking in through food and drink more than the body burns up through work or exercise. This excess energy is stored as subcutaneous fat. Conversely, losing weight results when the amount of energy expended by the body is more than the potential energy taken in, with the body making up the difference by borrowing the insufficient amount from stored body fat. The result is a reduction in body weight.

All this would seem to say, then, that to lose weight, one need only reduce the amount of food consumed. Fasting, or any such drastic reduction in the amount of food eaten would, of course, result in a rapid loss of body weight. Yet it is hardly possible that the delicate mechanisms of the body would be maintained if there is a nutritional deficiency in the quality of the food that is consumed. Our bodies are, after all, built from what we eat. To lose weight and still maintain one's health means, then, that the body's expenditure of energy should be increased in a positive way and the intake of food should be restricted while at the same time making certain that nutritional needs are being met. Taking in nutritive substances efficiently while on a low-energy diet requires that a person have a knowledge of basic nutrition and cooking techniques. For this latter point a few guidelines would be:

- Minimize nutritional loss by preparing nutritious foods quickly.
- Resolve the problem of likes and dislikes by devising ways of flavoring and seasoning foods.
- Prepare and serve low-calorie food in ways that please the eye as well as the palate while giving the appearance of plenty.

Eating Meals Regularly During the Day

There is a tendency to think that if a person skips breakfast or lunch, eating only two instead of three meals a day, the quantity of food consumed will decrease and he or she will become thin. This pattern, however, far from resulting in weight loss, can actually lead to being overweight. When the interval between meals is long, efficiency of food utilization is elevated, digestion and absorption of food take place more completely, and, as a consequence, food tends to be stored in the body as fat. Therefore, when trying to lose weight, it is sound policy to eat three meals a day. Have a hearty breakfast and lunch but go lightly on the evening meal, as people usually are less active after dinner than after lunch. Also, if there is food in the stomach when retiring, it is apt to be converted to fat and stored by the body during sleep, leading to an increase in weight. It is ideal, therefore, to take a low-calorie, light dinner centered on protein-rich foods.

Making 1600 Calories per Day the Basic Standard

The amount of energy necessary per day differs for each person according to sex, age, height, level of activity, and so on. Nevertheless, a standard can be established and each person can adjust the quantity according to his or her particular situation.

The standard we introduce here is a pattern of 1600 calories per day, a figure which represents the lowest level of food intake necessary for a housewife working around the house. If a person takes in a combination of foods like those shown in the chart on the next page, the daily nutritive needs of the body (protein, fat, carbohydrates, minerals and vitamins) will be basically met. This pattern has not been devised solely for those who wish to reduce; rather, it is a pattern that can be easily followed on a daily basis by anyone striving to maintain health and vitality. Since it is only a standard, a certain amount of flexibility in the calorie count is possible.

How to Choose Food Items for a Diet of 1600 Calories per Day *

Nutritional features	Food categories	Example with recommended amount	Weight = net weight
Necessary items			
To achieve balanced nutrition Good-quality protein Fats Calcium Vitamin B$_2$	Milk, milk products Eggs	Milk Chicken eggs	10 oz (300g) 2 oz (50g) (one)
To build tissue and blood Good-quality protein Fats Vitamins B$_1$, B$_2$ Calcium	Fish, shellfish, meat Beans, bean products	Sole fillet Round of beef Tofu	2 oz (50g) 2 oz (50g) 4 oz (100g) (⅓ block)
To maintain body's proper functioning Vitamins A, C Minerals Dietary fiber	Green leafy, yellow or red vegetables Other vegetables Tubers Fruit	Spinach, carrot Cabbage, celery Potato, sweet potato Any kind	4 oz (100g) 7 oz (200g) 4 oz (100g) 7 oz (200g)
Items the intake of which can be increased or decreased			
To build strength and maintain body temperature Carbohydrates Fats	Grains Sugar Oils and solid fats	Bread or plain rice Sugar Vegetable oil, butter	8¾ oz (240g) (4 slices) 1 lb (450g) (3 bowls) ¾ oz (20g) ¾ oz (20g)

Chart prepared by Women's College of Nutrition in Tokyo

For people who do not show much effect from a reduced intake of food, another possibility would be to cut down on the amount of grains, sugar, and fats consumed. Since the majority of overweight people take in enough food per day to generate more than 1600 calories anyway, the mere adoption of such a standard should result in a drop in weight.

In concrete terms, what kind of food should be included in a 1600-calorie diet? Looking at the menu plan on pages 108-110, you will undoubtedly be surprised at the large number of food products it is possible to take in in one day. The variety of items is indeed very rich. Readers are invited to utilize these sample menus as a starting point in devising their own plans.

Setting a Standard of 1 to 2 pounds (0.5 to 1.0 kilograms) Loss in Weight per Week

When people drastically reduce their food intake in the hope of losing even a little weight, there is likely to be a shortage of necessary nutrients and damage to the health. There may very well be a drop in weight, but the complexion will suffer, the skin will be rough, and the hair will become dull and lifeless.

Moreover, people are more likely to be irritable and suffer a decrease in spirit and vitality. It follows, then, that the best way to lose pounds sensibly is to steadfastly take in the necessary nutrients and decrease the weight a little at a time. To do this attractively and in a healthful way, a slow rate of about 1 to 2 pounds (0.5 to 1.0 kilograms) a week is ideal.

---

*Throughout the book, the term "calories" refers to kilocalories.

Sample Dieter's Menu

In this section, we show how to prepare a menu plan based on the principle of a nutritionally balanced diet of 1600 calories per day, mentioned on the previous two pages.

On this page and the following two pages, you will find a sample one-week menu of three meals daily which was constructed to provide 1600 calories per day. It is a diversified plan which incorporates both Japanese and Western dishes, is nutritionally balanced and contains dishes pleasing to the palate. We are sure you will want to refer to it to see how delicious meals can be enjoyed on just 1600 calories per day and how Japanese dishes are combined together.

All of the Japanese dishes introduced in this menu plan are dishes contained in this book. For your convenience, we have printed the names of these recipes in bold type and have inserted their page numbers in parentheses next to the name. All of the Western dishes introduced in this menu plan are simple dishes prepared in the average home. We have included in parentheses the ingredients for these dishes and their quantities. These numerical values were provided for the purpose of calculating the number of calories per meal and to give an indication of the number of calories typical Western breakfast-lunch foods contain.

When reducing or increasing the quantity of bread or rice to be eaten when they are used as staples, it is a good idea to keep in mind a standard measure. In the menu plan introduced here, we have made calculations as follows.

1 slice bread of 2¼ oz (60g) → 160 cal
Plain rice (6 oz or 150g (about 1 Japanese rice-bowlful)) → 200 cal

Monday

Breakfast	Buttered toast (1 slice or 2¼ oz (60g) bread, ½ tablespoon butter) Soft-boiled egg (1 egg) Wedge of cheese (1 ounce or 30g natural cheese) Coffee or tea with milk (large coffee or tea with ¾ cup or 150cc milk added) Fruit (6 oz or 150g of your choice) 592 cal
Lunch	**Rice topped with beef** (reduce the quantity of rice by one-half) *(page 16)* ***Miso* soup with *tofu* and *Shiitake* mushrooms** *(page 23)* **Quickly pickled vegetables** *(page 78)* 559 cal
Dinner	**Fish baked with vegetables in aluminum foil** *(page 59)* **Salad of hard-shelled clams with *miso* dressing** *(page 71)* **Squash boiled with flavorings** *(page 82)* **Japanese egg-drop soup with chicken and carrot** *(page 22)* Plain rice (3 oz or 80g (about ½ Japanese rice-bowlful)) 468 cal
Total Calories per Day	1619 cal

Notes: Breakfast includes the popular toast and boiled egg. Since hot toast soaks up butter like a sponge, check the quantity of butter carefully. Breads which have good fragrance and flavor, such as whole-wheat, rye, and French, will still be delicious if eaten plain without butter or jam.

Soft-boiled or poached eggs require no oil for cooking, digest more easily than fried ones and are less dry than plain hard-boiled eggs.

Cooking with aluminum foil is a good method for dieters. Foil locks in the flavor of ingredients, and oil or high-calorie seasonings are not needed. Try using chicken, salmon or shellfish also.

Tuesday

Cereal (1 oz or 25g cereal, 1 cup or 200cc
   milk, 1 teaspoon sugar)
Scrambled egg with spinach and
   tomato (1 oz or 25g spinach, 2 oz or
   50g tomato, 1 egg, salt, pepper,
   ½ tablespoon butter or oil)
Fresh orange juice (7 oz (200g) or about
   1 orange squeezed)

440 cal

Grilled Cheese (1 slice or 2¼ oz (60g)
   bread, ¾ oz or 20g processed cheese,
   ½ tablespoon butter)
Salad of tuna and *wakame* with soy
   sauce dressing *(page 70)*
1 cup American-style coffee

504 cal

Deep-fried marinated chicken
   (page 43)
Salad of bean sprouts with vinegar
   dressing *(page 78)*
Rice cooked with green peas (reduce
   the quantity of rice by one-half)
   (page 18)
Clear soup with shrimp and *okra*
   (page 22)

657 cal

1601 cal

Cereals are high in bulk. Adding milk,
a nutritionally excellent product, greatly
enhances the dish's value. Avoid sugar-
added packaged varieties.

Fresh orange juice has an abundance of vitamin C and helps awaken
the sleeping stomach. You might instead
just eat plain some fruit of your choice.

Deep-fried food is the main dish for
the evening meal. The side dishes do not
include any salad or sautéed items
which generally require oil. Using vinegared dishes and boiled vegetable
dishes with seasonings added makes
this a low-calorie meal.

Wednesday

Danish sweet roll
Café au lait or tea with milk (coffee or
   tea with ¾ cup or 150cc milk added)
Fruited yoghurt salad (2 oz or 50g plain
   yoghurt, 1 oz or 25g kiwi fruit, 2 oz or
   50g apple, 1 oz or 25g lettuce)

440 cal

Noodles cooked with chicken and
   vegetables (reduce the quantity of
   noodles by one-half) *(page 95)*
Sweet potatoes boiled with lemon
   flavoring *(page 87)*

620 cal

Salmon-*tofu* balls *(page 67)*
Boiled spinach with sesame seed
   dressing *(page 79)*
Miso soup with pork and scallions
   (page 23)
Plain rice (3 oz or 80g (about ½ Japanese
   rice-bowlful))

594 cal

1654 cal

Since it is easy to overeat noodles
and other pasta, one should add a lot
of vegetables, meat and seafood to the
dish and reduce the ratio of pasta.

The degree of oil absorption by
deep-fried foods differs according to
type of coating used. Arranged by
degree of oil absorption from lowest to
highest are items fried without coating,
items fried with bread crumb coating,
and items such as *tempura*, deep-fried
with batter.

Thursday

Same as breakfast for Monday

592 cal

Spaghetti with clam sauce (2¼ oz or
   60g dried spaghetti, 7 oz or 200g
   clams, ⅔ tablespoon olive oil, white
   wine, garlic, salt, pepper, and parsley,
   all in small amounts)
Japanese-style vegetable soup
   (page 27)
Garden salad (1 oz or 25g celery, 1 oz
   or 25g cucumber, ¾ oz or 20g carrot,
   1 oz or 25g long white radish, *miso*-
   mayonnaise dressing (½ tablespoon
   mayonnaise and 1 teaspoon *miso*)

545 cal

Rolled beef with vegetables *(page 51)*
Salad of asparagus and chicken with
   mustard dressing *(page 79)*
Miso soup with *wakame* (page 23,
   variation of *miso* soups)
Plain rice (4 oz or 100g (about 1 light
   Japanese rice-bowlful))
Fruit (4 oz or 100g of your choice)

477 cal

1614 cal

Serving the hard-shelled clams in
their shells on top of the spaghetti will
make the volume of the dish seem larger
and give the eater a feeling of
satisfaction.

Oils with strong fragrance or taste,
such as olive or sesame oil, can greatly
enhance the flavor of dishes even when
a small amount is used.

When making the *miso* soup with
wakame (a kind of seaweed), cut the
wakame into bite-sized pieces after
soaking and cook in the soup for a few
seconds, then flavor soup with *miso*.
Just after the soup boils again, turn off
the heat. *Wakame* has no calories. It can
be used, therefore, to add volume to
soups and salads.

Friday

Cereal (1 oz or 25g cereal, 1 cup or 200cc
    milk, 1 teaspoon sugar)
Buttered toast (1 slice or 2¼ oz (60g)
    bread, ½ tablespoon butter)
Fresh orange juice (7 oz (200g) or about
    1 orange squeezed)

487 cal

Beef, potatoes and onions cooked with
    flavorings *(page 50)*
Fresh *tofu* with condiments *(page 90)*
Quickly pickled vegetables *(page 78)*
Plain rice (3 oz or 80g (about ½ Japanese
    rice-bowlful))

572 cal

Tempura (reduce quantity by one-half)
    (page 62)
Steamed custard with chicken, shrimp
    and vegetables *(page 94)*
Long white radish and carrot
    marinated in vinegary sauce
    (page 79)

587 cal

1646 cal

Saturday

Grapefruit (½ medium)
2 bran muffins (2⅜ inches or 6cm in size)
    with 2 tablespoons jam
Coffee or tea with milk (½ cup or 100cc)

440 cal

Rice topped with ground chicken,
    eggs and green peas (reduce the
    quantity of rice by one-half) *(page 16)*
Clear soup with *tofu* *(page 22,* variation
    of clear soups)
Boiled spinach with sesame seed
    dressing *(page 79)*

578 cal

Boiled pork with Japanese-style sauce
    (reduce quantity of pork by one-half; eat
    with mustard sauce) *(page 55)*
Vegetables and chicken cooked with
    flavorings *(page 82)*
Salad of bean sprouts with soy sauce
    dressing *(page 78)*
Clear soup with clams *(page 22)*

580 cal

1598 cal

Sunday

Pancakes (1 egg, ⅓ cup or 70cc milk, 2¾ oz.
    or 70g flour, 1 teaspoon baking powder, a
    little sugar, a little vanilla extract, 1
    tablespoon butter), 2½ tablespoons
    butter and ½ cup or 100cc table syrup
1 cup American coffee with ¼ cup or
    50cc milk

816 cal

Sukiyaki (page 30)
Salad of crab and *wakame* with vinegar
    dressing *(page 70)*
Plain rice (6 oz or 150g (about 1 Japanese
    rice-bowlful))

771 cal

1587 cal

Tofu is a great diet dish. Served fresh with condiments, it is especially simple to prepare. In cold weather, try serving it hot by heating it in hot water to which *konbu* (dried kelp) has been added. For an interesting *tofu* "salad," top *tofu* with salad vegetables then pour over it the dressing used for the bean sprout salad on page 78.

Tempura is delicious, but the batter and deep-frying cause calories to rise steeply. Use caution concerning quantity and type of items consumed. Those that contract when deep-fried, such as squid, shrimp, and onions, absorb a smaller amount of oil, while items such as eggplant and mushrooms absorb oil like a sponge.

The quantity of rice in the rice dish at lunch is the key point to watch.

For the clear soup with *tofu*, add 2 ounces (50g) of *tofu* per person immediately after flavoring soup with salt and soy sauce. Bring soup to a·boil again, add the finely cut long green onion and turn off heat.

If the quantity of pork in the diner's dish is cut in half and vegetables added as complement, the meal can still satisfy the appetite. No staple is needed since the meal contains a potato.

On this holiday, for a change of pace, we have brunch, combining breakfast and lunch. Today we can enjoy something which takes more time and trouble, such as a pancake or crepe.

With *sukiyaki* and other one-pot table cooking, it is easy to lose track of how much has been eaten. Since it is troublesome to check all things you eat, just count the number of high-calorie foods eaten. You may, however, indulge freely in low-calorie foods, such as *shirataki* noodles and vegetables.

For dinner, you may opt to skip the staple (rice) if you are already full.

How to Entertain with Japanese Dishes

Begin Simply

First select one dish and work it in among your Western party dishes. Choose one that has very fresh and colorful ingredients and brightens up your table. On succeeding occasions, gradually increase the number of Japanese dishes until you find yourself tackling an all-Japanese meal.

For those unfamiliar with traditional patterns in the combining of Japanese dishes, use the menu plan presented on pages 108-110.

The items in the plan were chosen not only to demonstrate how to combine dishes but also for their contribution to the overall nutritional balance of the meals. Using the recipes in this book, four sample party meals (pages 111-115) have been put together for your reference.

The text, in addition to explaining how to combine dishes, also gives suggestions on the order in which they should be prepared and served. Using all these as a guide, you can work up your own menus keyed to your particular guests.

Deciding on the Main Dish First

Select one dish, taking into consideration the ages and preferences of your guests, purpose of the party, and the time of day and season the party will be held. You cannot go wrong if you choose a dish you have made many times before, one that is tasty, can be prepared with a minimum of fuss and about which you feel confident.

Deciding on the Side Dishes

Considering the likes and dislikes of your guests, decide on the side dishes, adjusting your selections on the basis of their contribution to the overall nutritional balance of the menu. It is important in Japanese cooking, though by no means limited to it, to try to achieve a harmony among sweet, spicy, sour and other tastes; foods with a light refreshing flavor are balanced against oily ones, cold against hot foods, and a few easy-to-prepare foods are served along with traditional ones requiring a long time to fix. Careful consideration, therefore, should be given to making up the menu.

Drinks and Desserts

The flavor of *sake* (rice wine), drunk hot or cold according to the season and type of food, is superb. A cup of hot Japanese green tea, served at the conclusion of the meal, is also important as a finishing touch. Aside from *sake*, other alcoholic beverages also go well with Japanese cooking. Beer, wine, whisky—in fact, almost any kind of drink is fine, and choice should be according to preference.

For dessert after a Japanese meal, fruit or homemade pastry goes well; as a matter of fact, a rich dessert after light, simple-tasting Japanese food is delectable indeed.

Serving Containers and Utensils

It is not necesary to think that just because Japanese food is being served one must use nothing but Japanese tableware. It is perfectly acceptable to use any party serviceware that you like, arranging the food on it so that it looks attractive and is easy to eat. When you simply wish to create a little Japanese atmosphere to go along with the food, you can add to your regular service small Japanese wares such as soy sauce containers, tiny plates, chopsticks and a tea set, all of which your guests will undoubtedly enjoy.

Hand-wrapped Sushi Dinner

Hand-wrapped *sushi* is an easy-to-make and informal *sushi* which each guest can enjoy making on his or her own just by wrapping rice and other ingredients inside a sheet of *nori* (dried laver). It is an especially good dish to serve when inviting close friends with whom you can relax. To accompany it, the clear soup with clams would be nice, as it has a flavor of high quality and is suitable for company. Cups of hot Japanese tea during and at the close of the meal are sure to please, also.

Points to Remember

Since hand-wrapped *sushi* is both the main dish and the chief food served, it would be sufficient to add only a clear soup to complete the menu. If you desire to add a side dish as well, it would be a plus for your menu to make it a vegetable dish, as there are few vegetables among the ingredients for *sushi*. A food with a strong, deep flavor or a dish which is lightly sweet would also go well with *sushi*. The variety of ingredients one could use in hand-wrapped *sushi* is large. This possibility for wide variation makes it a deluxe dish and allows you to increase or decrease items as you see fit.

Order of Preparation

- Things That Can be Done on the Day Before the Party
1. Prepare and store the vegetables and chicken cooked with flavorings. Making it a day ahead enhances the flavor.
2. Pickle the ginger. Ready-made ginger, if available, would save time.
3. Fry the egg, enclose it in plastic wrap without cutting, put it in an airtight container and refrigerate. (This step can be done on the day of the party also.)
4. Put the fresh clams in cold salt water and store in a cool, dark place to make them spew the sand.

- Things to Do on the Day of the Party
1. On the morning of the day of the party, but not fewer than three hours prior to its start, rinse the rice and drain in a colander. After it has drained for an hour, boil it and make "*sushi* rice." Cover the cooked rice with a damp dishcloth to keep it from drying out and set it aside at room temperature. *Do not refrigerate,* as this will make it dry and hard.
2. Wash and drain the vegetables to be used in the *sushi*.
3. Reheat the vegetable and chicken dish and put it into one large bowl or individual small ones. This dish is delicious even after it has cooled off.
4. Arrange on a platter the ingredients to be wrapped in the *nori,* cover them with plastic wrap or aluminum foil, and store in the refrigerator. (The *sashimi* and raw vegetables will lose their freshness if cut too early and should be prepared and arranged as close to serving time as possible.)
5. Cut the toasted *nori*. If exposed to the air for a long time after being cut, *nori* will wilt; it should, therefore, be kept in an airtight can or bag until just before serving, then toasted, cut and piled on a serving dish.
6. Prepare the clear soup with clams.

Serving Order
1. Place on the table (a) the large platter containing the ingredients to be wrapped inside the *nori,* (b) the rice in its container (or in two containers if the number of persons is large), along with spoons, (c) the plate for the *nori,* (d) a soy sauce holder, and (e) a small plate for each person to use for dipping the wrapped *sushi* into the soy sauce.
2. Set out the bowl containing the vegetables and chicken. If one large bowl is used, individual eating containers should be provided.
3. Dish up and serve the hot soup in individual bowls, and let the party begin.

Grilled Foods Dinner

At a party centered around a table-top grill, each person is his or her own cook, frying his or her favorite ingredients and flavoring them with Japanese-style dips: either sesame seed sauce or *ponzu* sauce or both. The *yakitori* can also be cooked on the grill, and everyone can enjoy its sizzling-hot excellence. Remember to provide your guests with paper aprons, and there'll be no worries about oil spatters.

Points to Remember

For the very reason that this kind of cooking requires little bother in the way of preparation you could, when using it for company, spend a little more time on extras, such as increasing the number of sauces or condiments. If *yakitori* is also going to be cooked at table, this will make for a wider range of flavors, and the activity around the table will seem more lively. Since food cooked on a grill has a rich, full-bodied taste, it is probably a good idea to serve one or two simple-to-make, light-tasting salads. An even simpler step would be to sliver some chilled vegetables and serve them as they are.

Order of Preparation

- Things That Can be Done on the Day Before the Party
  Cut the vegetables to be pickled, place them in the pickling solution, put a weight on top, and refrigerate. (This step can also be done on the day of the party, but it is probably better to do it a day ahead of time as pickling requires at least half a day.)
- Things to Do on the Day of the Party
1. Make the sesame, *ponzu,* and *yakitori* sauces.
2. Get started on the *yakitori* by cutting and skewering the meat and vegetables.
3. Cut the vegetables for grilling and place them on a large platter. Parboil the sweet potatoes, white potatoes, corn and carrot.

4. Prepare the meat and seafood for grilling and place on a large platter.
5. Prepare the condiments (grated radish, long scallion sliced paper-thin crosswise, wedged lemon, *shichimi togarashi* and mustard).
6. Lightly squeeze the pickled vegetables to remove pickling solution, and put them into a large rice tub or bowl.
7. Prepare the bean-sprout salad and put it into a large rice tub or bowl.
8. One hour before the party, rinse the rice, let it soak for 30 minutes, then cook. As an alternative, form the cooked rice into rice balls beforehand, wrap in aluminum foil to prevent drying, and serve as they are. This adds to the convenience and makes them easy to eat. They are also delicious left in the foil and reheated on top of the grill.

Serving Order

1. Prepare the grill, put out on the table the large platters piled with food, the small individual plates, and the sauces and condiments.
2. Put the pickled vegetables and bean-sprout salad on a serving tray and bring it to the table.
3. Begin to fry. With the *yakitori*, first fry it a little as it is, then dip it in the *yakitori* sauce and fry it a little longer.
4. Serve the cooked rice in bowls or, if formed into balls, in the foil. Bread may be served in place of rice.

Buffet Party (A)

This deluxe menu makes possible the enjoyment of a number of very different dishes. It is high in volume and centers on the deep-fried marinated chicken. The *sashimi*-style beef (item 3 above), ideal as an hors d'oeuvre, can be cut into individual-sized pieces and placed on a large platter so that it is easy for guests to pick up. Also, depending on the number of guests and how well the preparations go, it might be a good idea to select only one or two of the three meat dishes suggested.

Points to Remember
Since you will want to serve the deep-fried chicken while it is still very hot, preparations for all the other dishes should be done first. Making and refrigerating the beef rolls a day ahead will shorten preparation time on the day of the party and make things go easier. When a large quantity of meat is served at a meal, it is nutritionally sound to serve a number of vegetable dishes along with it. You might, for example, serve a salad containing generous amounts of *wakame*, a noncaloric health food. Also, the inclusion of a sweet-tasting item such as the lemon-flavored sweet potatoes will add an interesting accent and liven up the meal.

Order of Preparation
- Things That Can be Done on the Day Before the Party
1. Make the rolled beef with vegetables, wrap them in foil whole without cutting them, put into airtight container and refrigerate. (This step can also be done on the day of the party.)
2. Make the *dashi* (fish stock) for the soup and refrigerate. (This step, too, can be done on the day of the party.)
- Things to Do on the Day of the Party
1. Make the lemon-flavored sweet potatoes.

2. Cook the beef for *sashimi,* wrap but do not cut it, then refrigerate until needed. (Cutting the beef immediately will result in the loss of its savory juices, so lock them in by cooking the beef quickly and refrigerating it right away.)
3. Marinate the chicken.
4. Wash the rice. After letting it soak for 30 minutes, boil it together with the green peas.
5. Make preliminary preparations for the clear soup. Cut the chicken and preflavor it. Cut, boil, and set aside the carrot.
6. Cut the beef rolls and place them in serving containers.
7. Cut the *sashimi*-style beef and place on a plate. (Cutting it into thin slices will make it easier to eat and give an appearance of larger volume.)
8. Make the tuna-*wakame* salad. Immediately before serving, mix in the dressing and put salad into a rice tub or large bowl.
9. Warm up the lemon-flavored sweet potatoes—or they can be served at room temperature—and put them into a rice tub or large bowl or into individual containers.
10. Make final preparations for the soup.
11. Deep-fry the chicken.

Serving Order
1. Set out the plates and chopsticks for the guests, and any other tableware necessary, then bring on the beef rolls, *sashimi*-style beef, tuna-*wakame* salad and lemon-flavored sweet potatoes.
2. Set out the rice with green peas and the soup.
3. Finally, put the deep-fried chicken on the table while piping hot.

Buffet Party (B)

This menu, which incorporates seafood and chicken, has simple, refreshing flavors. The two salmon dishes, which must certainly be considered the main dishes of this menu, are combined with highly recommended items popular with old and young alike. *Sake* (rice wine) is also recommended with this menu. If you wish, you may select either the crab or carrot salad, or substitute plain white rice or bread for the rice cooked with chicken and vegetables.

Points to Remember

The quantity of food per dish in this menu is not large. If the party is for a large number of guests, you will need to increase the number of dishes served. You can, of course, increase the quantity per dish also. In this menu you will find items that can be made ahead of time and set aside, thus freeing you on the day of the party, as well as items which, even when cold, retain their goodness. It might be a good idea to consider putting out the deep-fried salmon balls after the party has begun. It might also be advantageous to put the cooked rice in a large container so that each guest can take the amount that discretion and appetite dictate.

Order of Preparation

• Things That Can be Done on the Day Before the Party

1. Make the vinegared radish and carrot dish and store in the refrigerator. (This task can also be done on the day of the party.) If made in advance, the flavor of the marinade will penetrate well.
2. Sauté the ground-chicken loaf, wrap in foil, place in an airtight container, and refrigerate. (This step, too, can be taken on the day of the party.)
3. Make the *dashi* (fish stock) for the soup and refrigerate. (This can also be done on the day of the party.)
4. Boil and store in the refrigerator the chicken and vegetables that will be the ingredients for the rice dish. (This step can also be done on the day of the party.)

• Things To Do on the Day of the Party

1. Prepare the boiled squash dish.
2. Coat the salmon with *teriyaki* sauce. Cutting the slices into two or three pieces will make them easier to eat.
3. Rinse the rice and soak in water for 30 minutes.
4. Make the ingredients for the deep-fried salmon-*tofu* balls into a paste, form the balls, and cover with a damp dishcloth to prevent drying out.
5. Make preliminary preparations for the clear soup. Do the advance preparations for the shrimp, then boil them. Cut the okra. Next, cut the lemon rind into very fine strips.
6. Cook the rice.
7. Prepare the crab salad with vinegar dressing, but do not mix in the dressing until just before serving.
8. Cook the salmon. Grate the radish just prior to placing it on the table.
9. Coat the salmon-*tofu* balls lightly with flour, adjust their shapes, then deep fry.
10. Make the clear soup.

Serving Order

1. Set out the plates and chopsticks for the guests, and any other tableware necessary, then follow that with the grilled salmon with *teriyaki* sauce (adding the grated radish); next, bring out the ground-chicken loaf, the crab salad, the vinegared radish and carrot dish, and the boiled pumpkin.
2. After the guests are seated, put out the rice with chicken and vegetables.
3. Finally, place the salmon-*tofu* balls on the table while still piping hot.

Composition of Major Ingredients Used in Japanese Cooking

Based on Standard Tables of Food Composition in Japan, fourth revised edition, 1982, Resources Council, Science and Technology Agency, Government of Japan

*As a principle, the names of foods are as they appear in the aforementioned document.

*In the tables, the numerical values are calculated on the basis of 100 grams of edible portion of food and, for convenience, are given also in terms of ¼ pound. These were calculated using a conversion value of 1 ounce equals 28.35 grams. Energy is expressed in calories, protein, fats, and carbohydrates in grams, and sodium in milligrams.

*Where the numerical value for food composition is indicated by a "0," the composition was either not included in the above document or was not given in terms which correspond to those used in this table. Where the quantity of a nutritional element was so small as to be insignificant, the table indicates this fact with the symbol "Ø." A dash (—) indicates cases where the composition was either not calculable or was unclear.

Food and description	Per 100g and ¼ lb of edible portion									
	Calories		Protein (g)		Fats (g)		Carbo-hydrates (g) (Nonfibrous)		Sodium (mg)	
	100g	¼ lb	100g	¼ lb	100g	¼ lb	100g	¼ lb	100g	¼ lb
GRAINS										
Rice, wetland paddy										
Brown, unpolished	351	398	7.4	8.4	3.0	3.4	71.8	81.4	2	2.3
White, polished	356	404	6.8	7.7	1.3	1.5	75.5	85.6	2	2.3
Wheat flour										
Soft, first grade (cake flour)	368	417	8.0	9.1	1.7	1.9	75.7	85.8	2	2.3
Medium, first grade (all-purpose)	368	417	9.0	10.2	1.8	2.0	74.6	84.6	2	2.3
Hard, first grade (bread flour)	366	415	11.7	13.3	1.8	2.0	71.4	81.0	2	2.3
Wheat noodles, Japanese-style (udon), raw										
Uncooked	280	318	6.8	7.7	1.3	1.5	57.0	64.6	600	680
Boiled	101	115	2.5	2.8	0.5	0.6	20.3	23.0	45	51.
Wheat noodles, Japanese-style, dried (hoshi-udon)										
Uncooked	358	406	8.9	10.1	1.8	2.0	72.3	82.0	1200	1361
Boiled	93	105	2.4	2.7	0.5	0.6	18.6	21.1	120	136
Wheat noodles, Japanese-style, dried, special varieties (somen, hiyamugi)										
Uncooked	363	412	9.7	11.0	1.9	2.2	72.4	82.1	1200	1361
Boiled	128	145	3.4	3.9	0.7	0.8	25.4	28.8	120	136
Buckwheat noodles (soba), raw										
Uncooked	274	311	9.8	11.1	1.9	2.2	54.2	61.5	1	1.1
Boiled	132	150	4.8	5.4	1.0	1.1	25.8	29.3	2	2.3
Buckwheat noodles, dried (hoshi-soba)										
Uncooked	360	408	13.6	15.4	2.6	2.9	70.2	79.6	2	2.3
Boiled	116	132	4.5	5.1	0.9	1.0	22.3	25.3	2	2.3
POTATOES AND STARCHES										
Sweet potatoes, raw	123	139	1.2	1.4	0.2	0.2	28.7	32.5	13	14.7
Potatoes, white (jaga-imo), raw	77	87	2.0	2.3	0.2	0.2	16.8	19.1	2	2.3
Taro, Japanese (sato-imo), raw	60	68	2.6	2.9	0.2	0.2	12.3	13.9	1	1.1
Starch, potato, white, powdered (katakuriko)	330	374	0.1	0.1	0.1	0.1	81.6	92.5	2	2.3
Starch, root called "devil's tongue"										
Block form (konnyaku)	—	—	0.1	0.1	0	0	2.2	2.5	10	11
Noodle form (shirataki)	—	—	0.2	0.2	0	0	2.9	3.3	10	11
Starch, Mung beans, noodle form (harusame)	345	391	0.2	0.2	0.4	0.5	84.6	95.9	16	18
SUGARS AND SWEETENERS										
Soft sugar, white, superior	384	435	0	0	0	0	99.2	112.5	2	2.3
FATS AND OILS										
Vegetable oils (average for blended oil)	921	1044	0	0	100.0	113.4	0	0	0	0
Margarine	759	861	0.3	0.3	82.1	93.1	0.5	0.6	800	907
Butter, salted	745	845	0.6	0.7	81.0	91.9	0.2	0.2	750	851
NUTS AND SEEDS										
Ginkgo nuts										
Raw	172	195	4.7	5.3	1.7	1.9	34.5	39.1	1	1.1
Boiled	165	187	4.3	4.9	1.3	1.5	34.0	38.6	3	3.4
Sesame seeds										
Dried	578	655	19.8	22.5	51.9	58.9	15.3	17.4	2	2.3
Roasted	599	679	20.3	23.0	54.2	61.5	15.3	17.4	2	2.3
PULSES (BEANS)										
Soybeans (Japanese), whole, dry	417	473	35.3	40.0	19.0	21.5	23.7	26.9	1	1.1
Bean curd (tofu)										
Cotton-strained (momen-goshi)	77	87	6.8	7.7	5.0	5.7	0.8	0.9	3	3.4

Food and description	Per 100g and ¼ lb of edible portion									
	Calories		Protein (g)		Fats (g)		Carbo-hydrates (g) (Nonfibrous)		Sodium (mg)	
	100g	¼ lb	100g	¼ lb	100g	¼ lb	100g	¼ lb	100g	¼ lb
Silk-strained (kinu-goshi)	58	66	5.0	5.7	3.3	3.7	1.7	1.9	4	4.5
Grilled (yaki-dofu)	88	100	7.8	8.8	5.7	6.5	1.0	1.1	4	4.5
Bean curd, thin deep-fried (abura-age)	388	440	18.6	21.1	33.1	37.5	2.8	3.2	10	11.3
Fermented soybean paste (miso)										
Rice malt-soybean paste (kome-koji-miso), sweet	217	246	9.7	11.0	3.0	3.4	36.7	41.6	2400	2722
Rice malt-soybean paste (kome-koji-miso), dark yellow	186	211	13.1	14.9	5.5	6.2	19.1	21.7	5100	5783
Barley malt-soybean paste (mugi-koji-miso)	198	225	9.7	11.0	4.3	4.9	28.3	32.1	4200	4763
Soybean malt-soybean paste (mame-koji-miso)	217	246	17.2	19.5	10.5	11.9	11.3	12.8	4300	4876
FISH AND SHELLFISH										
Sardines (ma-iwashi), raw	213	242	19.2	21.8	13.8	15.6	0.5	0.6	360	408
Bonito (katsuo), raw	129	146	25.8	29.3	2.0	2.3	0.4	0.5	44	50
Salmon (sake), raw	167	189	20.7	23.5	8.4	9.5	0.1	0.1	95	108
Mackerel (saba), raw	239	271	19.8	22.5	16.5	18.7	0.1	0.1	80	91
Sea bream, red (ma-dai), raw	112	127	19.0	21.5	3.4	3.9	0	0	70	79
Codfish (tara), raw	70	79	15.7	17.8	0.4	0.5	Ø	Ø	130	147
Yellowtail (buri), raw	257	291	21.4	24.3	17.6	20.0	0.3	0.3	32	36
Tuna, blue-black (kuro-maguro), raw										
Lean meat	133	151	28.3	32.1	1.4	1.6	0.1	0.1	50	57
Oily meat (toro)	322	365	21.4	24.3	24.6	27.9	0.1	0.1	43	49
Hard-shelled clams (asari), raw	49	56	8.3	9.4	1.0	1.1	1.2	1.4	400	454
Clams (hamaguri), raw (quahogs)	60	68	10.4	11.8	0.9	1.0	1.9	2.2	500	567
Scallops (hotategai), raw	77	87	13.8	15.6	1.2	1.4	1.8	2.0	250	284
Squid (ika), raw	76	86	15.6	17.7	1.0	1.1	0.1	0.1	200	227
Prawns, tiger (kuruma-ebi), raw (shrimp)	93	105	20.5	23.2	0.7	0.8	Ø	Ø	140	159
Crab (ke-gani), raw	82	93	18.8	21.3	0.3	0.3	Ø	Ø	260	295
Octopus (tako), raw	76	86	16.4	18.6	0.7	0.8	0.1	0.1	280	318
Fish paste cakes, block form (kamaboko), steamed	98	111	12.0	13.6	0.9	1.0	9.7	11.0	1000	1134
Fish paste cakes, stick form (chikuwa), grilled	126	143	12.2	13.8	2.1	2.4	13.5	15.3	1000	1134
MEATS (cuts vary in different countries)										
Beef (with fat attached)										
—(chuck, total edible)										
Japanese cattle (wa-gyu)	233	264	18.3	20.8	16.4	18.6	0.3	0.3	60	68
Dairy-fattened steer	184	209	19.0	21.5	10.9	12.4	0.3	0.3	60	68
—(chuck loin, total edible)										
Japanese cattle	328	372	16.2	18.4	27.5	31.2	0.3	0.3	40	45
Dairy-fattened steer	238	270	18.5	21.0	16.9	19.2	0.2	0.2	55	62
—(rib loin, total edible)										
Japanese cattle	357	405	15.6	17.7	30.8	34.9	0.3	0.3	42	48
Dairy-fattened steer	262	297	18.2	20.6	19.6	22.2	0.3	0.3	50	57
—(sirloin, total edible)										
Japanese cattle	364	413	16.9	19.2	31.0	35.2	0.3	0.3	55	62
Dairy-fattened steer	236	268	18.5	21.0	16.6	18.8	0.3	0.3	50	57
—(flank, plate, total edible)										
Japanese cattle	317	359	16.1	18.3	26.4	29.9	0.2	0.2	45	51
Dairy-fattened steer	260	295	17.8	20.2	19.6	22.2	0.2	0.2	50	57
—(inside round, total edible)										
Japanese cattle	165	187	21.5	24.4	7.6	8.6	0.7	0.8	55	62
Dairy-fattened steer	148	168	21.2	24.0	6.1	6.9	0.3	0.3	60	68
—(outside round, total edible)										
Japanese cattle	187	212	19.6	22.2	10.9	12.4	0.5	0.6	50	57
Dairy-fattened steer	155	176	21.2	24.0	6.8	7.7	0.3	0.3	44	50
—(rump, total edible)										
Japanese cattle	237	269	18.1	20.5	16.8	19.1	0.6	0.7	50	57
Dairy-fattened steer	203	230	18.6	21.1	13.0	14.7	0.5	0.6	47	53
—(fillet)										
Japanese cattle	232	263	19.5	22.1	15.7	17.8	0.5	0.6	45	51
Dairy-fattened steer	155	176	21.4	24.3	6.7	7.6	0.3	0.3	50	57

Food and description	Calories		Protein (g)		Fats (g)		Carbo-hydrates (g) (Nonfibrous)		Sodium (mg)	
	100g	¼ lb	100g	¼ lb	100g	¼ lb	100g	¼ lb	100g	¼ lb
Chicken (meat with fat attached)										
—(wing, broiler)	221	251	17.2	19.5	15.8	18.0	Ø	Ø	80	91
—(breast, total edible, broiler)	203	230	20.6	23.4	12.3	13.9	0.2	0.2	30	34
—(thigh, broiler)	211	239	17.3	19.6	14.6	16.6	0.1	0.1	45	51
—(chicken breast fillet (sasami), broiler)	105	119	23.7	26.9	0.5	0.6	0.1	0.1	30	34
Pork (with fat attached)										
—(picnic shoulder, total edible, large-type breeds)	217	246	17.5	19.8	15.1	17.1	0.3	0.3	50	57
—(Boston butt, total edible, large-type breeds)	283	321	16.4	18.6	22.6	25.6	0.2	0.2	40	45
—(loin, total edible, large-type breeds)	314	356	16.5	18.7	25.7	29.1	0.5	0.6	40	45
—(belly, total edible, large-type breeds)	417	473	13.2	15.0	38.3	43.4	0.3	0.3	39	44
—(inside ham, total edible, large-type breeds)	158	179	20.4	23.1	7.4	8.4	0.5	0.6	31	35
—(outside ham, total edible, large-type breeds)	233	264	17.8	20.2	16.6	18.8	0.4	0.5	50	57
—(fillet, large-type breeds)	134	152	21.5	24.4	4.5	5.1	0.3	0.3	40	45
VEGETABLES										
Chinese cabbage (hakusai), raw	12	14	1.1	1.2	0.1	0.1	1.9	2.2	5	5.7
Eggplant (nasu), raw	18	20	1.1	1.2	0.1	0.1	3.4	3.9	1	1.1
Cucumber, Japanese-type (kyuri), meat, raw	11	12	1.0	1.1	0.2	0.2	1.6	1.8	2	2.3
Long scallions (negi)										
white part	27	31	1.1	1.2	0.1	0.1	5.9	6.7	1	1.1
green part	25	28	1.7	1.9	0.2	0.2	4.6	5.2	1	1.1
Regular scallions (wakegi), leaves, raw	36	41	1.9	2.2	Ø	Ø	8.0	9.1	1	1.1
Chives (asatsuki), green parts, raw	28	32	2.5	2.8	0.1	0.1	4.7	5.3	1	1.1
Radish, long white (daikon), raw	18	20	0.8	0.9	0.1	0.1	3.4	3.9	14	16
Burdock root (gobo), raw	76	86	2.8	3.2	0.1	0.1	16.2	18.4	6	6.8
Lotus root (renkon), raw	66	75	2.1	2.4	Ø	Ø	15.1	17.1	28	32
Bamboo shoots (takenoko), raw	34	39	3.6	4.1	0.1	0.1	6.0	6.8	Ø	Ø
Trefoil (mitsuba), leafstalk and leaves, raw	19	22	1.0	1.1	0.1	0.1	3.5	4.0	8	9.1
Snow peas (saya-endo), pods, raw	31	35	3.2	3.6	0.1	0.1	5.5	6.2	1	1.1
Pumpkin, Japanese-type (kabocha), raw (winter squash)	36	41	1.3	1.5	0.1	0.1	7.9	8.9	1	1.1
Sweet potatoes ⎫										
Japanese taro ⎬ See POTATOES AND STARCHES										
White potatoes ⎭										
Beefsteak plant (perilla), leaves (shiso)	35	40	3.8	4.3	0.1	0.1	5.5	6.2	1	1.1
Ginger root (shoga)										
Raw	31	35	0.9	1.0	0.1	0.1	6.3	7.1	4	4.5
Pickled	35	40	0.5	0.6	0.1	0.1	7.5	8.5	370	420
Red pepper (togarashi), excluding seeds, dried	328	372	14.0	16.0	11.4	12.9	23.1	26.2	16	18
Gourd strips, dried (kampyo)	264	299	7.1	8.1	0.2	0.2	59.8	67.8	3	3.4
FUNGI										
Shiitake mushrooms										
Raw	—	—	2.0	2.3	0.3	0.3	5.3	6.0	3	3.4
Dried (Chinese black)	—	—	20.3	23.0	3.4	3.9	52.9	60.0	19	22
ALGAE										
Laver										
Dried (nori)	—	—	38.8	44.0	1.9	2.2	39.5	44.8	120	136
Toasted (yaki-nori)	—	—	40.9	46.4	2.0	2.3	41.7	47.3	130	136
Seasoned and dried (ajitsuke-nori)	—	—	38.4	43.5	2.8	3.2	39.7	45.0	2200	2495
Kelp, dried (konbu)	—	—	8.0	9.1	2.0	2.3	54.3	61.6	2700	3062
Seaweed, a variety (wakame)										
Raw	—	—	1.9	2.2	0.2	0.2	3.8	4.3	610	692
Dried	—	—	15.0	17.0	3.2	3.6	35.3	40.0	6100	6917
SEASONINGS AND SPICES										
Soy sauce (shoyu)										
Dark (koi-kuchi)	58	66	7.5	8.5	Ø	Ø	7.1	8.1	5900	6691
Light (usu-kuchi)	48	54	5.7	6.5	Ø	Ø	6.3	7.1	6400	7258
Sashimi-use (tamari)	76	86	10.0	11.3	Ø	Ø	9.0	10.2	5900	6691
Vinegar (su)	32	36	0.2	0.2	0	0	5.0	5.7	290	329
Rice wine, refined (seishu or sake), second class	106	120	0.4	0.5	Ø	Ø	5.0	5.7	2	2.3
Rice wine, cooking-use (mirin)	236	268	0.4	0.5	Ø	Ø	41.9	47.5	1	1.1
Horseradish, Japanese, powdered (wasabi)	332	376	11.4	13.0	1.1	1.2	69.0	78.2	30	34
Japanese prickly ash, seed pods, powdered (sansho)	—	—	10.3	11.7	6.2	7.0	49.7	56.4	10	11

Index